A HANDBOOK FOR TEENS
WHO LIKE TO WRITE

A HANDBOOK FOR TEENS
WHO LIKE TO WRITE

VICTORIA HANLEY

PRUFROCK PRESS INC.
WACO, TEXAS

Library of Congress Control Number: 2008921084

Copyright © 2008, 2012 Prufrock Press Inc.

Cover art by Zach Howard

ISBN-13: 978-1-877673-81-8

Prufrock Press Inc.
P.O. Box 8813
Waco, TX 76714-8813
Phone: (800) 998-2208
Fax: (800) 240-0333
http://www.prufrock.com

To the young writers of today—
who will write the stories of tomorrow.

And to James Hathaway, Charli O'Dell,
and teachers like them.

TABLE OF CONTENTS

Chapter One: Freeing Your Imagination 1

Chapter Two: Creating Characters 7

Chapter Three: Beginnings 31

Chapter Four: Setting 37

Chapter Five: The Heart of a Writer 51

Chapter Six: Writing Dialogue 61

Chapter Seven: Showing and Telling 77

Chapter Eight: Plotting and Scheming 83

Chapter Nine: Conflicts, Middles, and Ends 91

Chapter Ten: Polishing Your Writing 103

Chapter Eleven: Point of View 115

Chapter Twelve: Into the Future 127

Chapter Thirteen: Interviews With Authors 131

Chapter Fourteen: Questions and Answers 175

Acknowledgments 185

Bibliography 187

About the Author 191

Index 193

Common Core State Standards Alignment 197

DEAR WRITER,

Your stories are all yours and waiting to be told.

If you've picked up this book, you're interested in creative writing. Maybe fascinating characters walk into your mind unannounced and beg you to write about them. Maybe you enjoy imagining the way things could be in a different world. Or maybe you're an avid reader, and curious about how authors do what they do.

Whatever your interest, and whether you're just setting out on your first storytelling journey or you've finished a draft of a whole novel, you can use *Seize the Story* as a handbook.

Before we begin, I should tell you that when I first tried writing a novel, I knew nothing about elements of fiction such as characterization, setting, dialogue, etc. Consequently, I got no farther than a few pages of my own book before getting stuck.

Up until then, I had avoided writing classes, believing they would ruin my creativity. I thought that if I studied writing techniques, then writing would start to feel methodical—more like doing dishes or folding laundry than creating art.

But then I noticed illustrators getting excited about learning brush strokes, actors taking classes on gesture and voice, and dancers studying how to bend, twist, and leap. And I remembered I hadn't learned to play the guitar without a little instruction and plenty of practice. Maybe learning the elements of fiction wouldn't be such a bad idea.

So I started checking out information on how to write and also went over some of my favorite novels to look at the way they were written.

It took me five years to write my first novel, *The Seer and the Sword*. It took so long because (a) I didn't know what I was doing, and (b) I was busy being a working mom. But I got it done, and learned a lot along the way. Two more novels and a nonfiction book followed, and now I'm published in thirteen languages.

This book spills the secrets I've learned about creative writing, and also some of the secrets of other authors who write for teens—T. A. Barron, Joan Bauer, Hilari Bell, Dia Calhoun, Chris Crutcher, Teresa R. Funke, Nancy Garden, Elise Leonard, David Lubar, Carolyn Meyer, Todd Mitchell, Lauren Myracle, Donita Paul, Stephanie Perkins, Olugbemisola Rhuday-Perkovich, Laura Resau, Lynda Sandoval, James Van Pelt, and Denise Vega.

Each chapter has suggestions for writing exercises. Some are easy while others are more complex. You might be the kind of person who likes to read through the book first and then choose whether to do the exercises, or you could be an over-achiever who does every exercise step by step and writes as much as you possibly can. The approach is up to you.

Stories flit and drift through our minds, but if we seize them, they change into something others can enjoy.

I hope you seize yours.

Victoria Hanley

FREEING YOUR IMAGINATION

CHAPTER ONE

FREEING YOUR IMAGINATION

What is now proved was once only imagined.
— William Blake

Anyone who has never made a mistake
has never tried anything new.
— Albert Einstein

All of the writing techniques in the world can't take the place of your imagination. It's your imagination that will give you your stories.

The more you use your imagination, the more it develops. As we go through *Seize the Story*, there will be many opportunities to open up your imagination. But one thing you can get started on immediately—and keep doing all your life—is freewriting.

Freewriting. Even ten minutes a day of freewriting can expand your imagination in a big way. By freewriting, I mean writing whatever comes to mind. Use good grammar or bad, be neat or very messy, write in a logical way, or make no sense at all. It's just you and the page, without criticism.

That's the only rule in freewriting: no criticism. None whatsoever. Your imagination needs a place to run free. Don't worry about mistakes because mistakes don't exist in freewriting. Don't grade yourself. Don't compare yourself to anyone else. Dream any dream, follow wild thoughts and heartfelt prayers, record things you want to remember, vent about things you'd like to forget, create poetry, practice your handwriting, or simply doodle. The content isn't important. The freedom is.

Try writing at different times. Set your alarm for ten minutes early and write while you're still half asleep. Take a little time the minute you get home from work or school. Write just before you drift off at the end of the day.

Getting Started With Freewriting

Here are a few prompts to get going with freewriting. Let whatever flows come forth from these beginnings.

I am…
I dream…
Today…
Down deep I know…

Write whatever comes to mind. If you can't think of anything, write "I can't think of anything," and go from there. Just keep writing until the ten minutes are up.

After a few weeks of daily freewriting your imagination will start to expand. When it does, you may be surprised—even if you were highly imaginative to begin with. The more you invite your creative mind to communicate, the more it will show you.

First drafts. When you begin to write a new story, you've got nothing but fresh space on your page. What could be better than that?

Ha!

Writer Gene Fowler said, "Writing is easy; all you do is sit staring at a blank sheet of paper until the drops of blood form on your forehead."

And he wasn't even writing horror.

Before writing a novel myself, I had the idea that authors are effortlessly filled with perfect stories. I thought their words began flowing on page one and only stopped flowing when the story was finished.

The truth? First drafts are terrible—at least mine are—and so are those of many other writers. Because of this, I dread starting a new book the way I'd dread living in the middle of an especially disturbing nightmare. Getting through that first draft feels very much like clawing my way through solid rock using only my fingernails.

I don't usually show people my first attempts at writing a scene, but I'll make an exception here. This is a small sample of a genuine first draft:

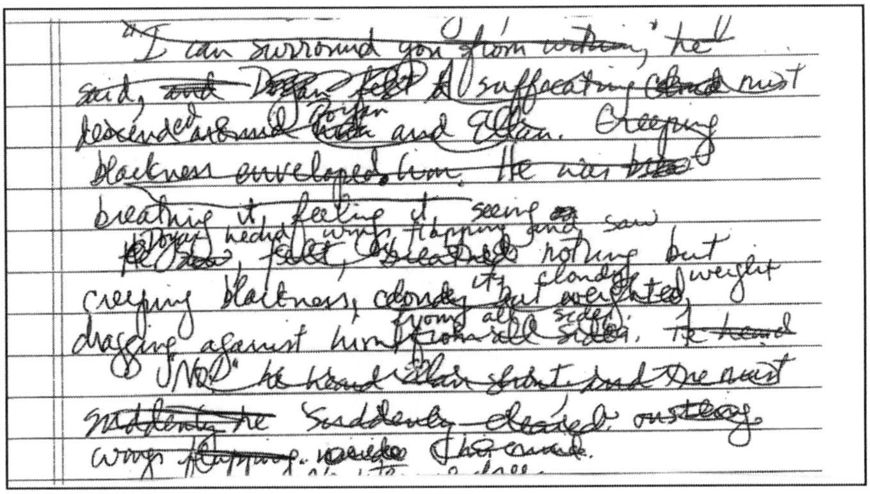

Well, at least I got a sentence out of it. "Dorjan heard wings flapping and saw nothing but creeping fog, a cloudy weight dragging against him" went into my novel *The Healer's Keep*. (If you can't read the handwritten sentence, don't worry. It's illegible.)

Not every handwritten page of a first draft is full of crossed-out lines. Sometimes almost a whole paragraph will work out fine and land in a book without having to be rewritten. Not often, though. I've frequently thrown away entire pages—even whole chapters. I tell you this so you won't beat yourself up if your own first drafts don't match up to your inner vision.

One good thing about first drafts: No one else has to see them as they make their way in murky splendor from the mists of your creative mind. And a first draft will get you to a second draft, which will be better.

I've tried to find a way around writing first drafts, but so far it appears that the only way to get through them is … to get through them. I've tried to jump from the first draft to the final draft, but that doesn't seem to work either. Once I have a handwritten first draft, I type it into the computer. Then I print it out and mark it up all over again. It usually takes about twelve drafts before my books are close to readable.

Not every writer does it this way—writers are very individual in how they do things. Some like to type their first drafts. Some like to write in the company of others. Some talk into a tape recorder. Some say, "Three drafts and that's enough."

Whatever works!

I admit I've met a few authors who say they love writing first drafts. Such people do exist. If you're one of them, and you thrill to the idea of a first draft, please ignore the preceding paragraphs.

But if you feel the weight of your unwritten story like a mountain of rock ready to crush you, a mountain where you're stuck until you dig your way out, I want you to know one thing: You're normal.

Either way, it's time to seize your story!

Even ten minutes a day of freewriting can expand your imagination in a big way.

CREATING CHARACTERS

CHAPTER TWO

CREATING CHARACTERS

**All the world's a stage,
and all the men and women merely players;
they have their exits and their entrances...**
— **William Shakespeare**

After reading Chapter One, you may be asking, "Isn't there anything *fun* about a first draft?"

Yes. Absolutely yes. There are characters to meet, characters who will lead you into the action of your story, characters you'll get to know like close friends, characters you'll come to love.

Where do fictional characters come from? It's hard to say, especially since different writers have different ideas about it. But I think characters are formed deep in the creative mind in the same place dreams are made.

I always feel a glow when new characters appear. Getting to know them is going to enliven my days for weeks, months, or even years. Does that sound strange? Story characters aren't real the way you and I are real—they come from the mind of the writer. So what do I mean by saying I'll get to know them? Aren't they already known?

Like the storybook Pinocchio—a wooden puppet who transformed into a real boy—fictional characters take on lives of their own, lives that seem real. They have surprising goals and motivations, hopes and fears, flaws and failings.

Many authors of fiction actually feel an imaginary character as a definite presence. I know I do. This doesn't interfere with my ability to function just fine in my daily life. I'm not talking about getting lost in delusion. I'm talking about working with fictional people as if they're believable. Real unto themselves. Alive, although imaginary.

If you don't see your fictional characters vividly in your mind's eye, that's all right. You may have a different writing style where characters reveal themselves to you in a more abstract way. There are as many ways to write as there are people writing, and it's not necessary to see your characters clearly in order to write about them.

But something *is* necessary for your characters to take their place in your story. Readers must care.

The first reader who must care is the writer. To take a deep interest in your characters, it helps to get to know them.

Meeting a *Character of Your Own*

Think of something you wish you had the nerve to say but haven't said. (If you're the sort of person who always says exactly what's on your mind, imagine a friend who has trouble saying certain things out loud.)

Now imagine a character who would have no problem saying what you haven't said but wish you could. Remember, there are no limits to what you can create in fiction. Your character can be anyone or anything at all, from the smallest pixie to the biggest dragon, from a disembodied spirit to a solid six-foot-tall man, from a time-traveling princess to a slave who belongs to a real period in history.

Give yourself a minute or two, and let the character begin to form in your mind. Take your time and don't force anything. You might see the character in your mind's eye. You might hear him or her talking in your creative ear. You might simply get a gut feeling for who the character is.

Sometimes it's helpful to let a character develop gradually over days or weeks. It's not always an instant process. And sometimes the character will just "appear" fully formed.

Interviewing Your Character

When you begin to have a clear sense of who your character might be, sit down and pretend to interview him or her. You can ask anything at all. Examples: Where do you live? How did you grow up? What are your best qualities? What are your flaws? What do you want? What problems are you facing?

Protagonists and antagonists. A leading character in fiction is known as a *protagonist*. Stories are centered around their protagonists.

Harry Potter is the protagonist of *Harry Potter and the Sorcerer's Stone* (J.K. Rowling). Elizabeth Bennett is the protagonist of *Pride and Prejudice* (Jane Austen). Katniss Everdeen is the protagonist of *The Hunger Games*. Most stories have one main protagonist, but it's possible to have more than one.

Antagonists work against protagonists, taking away what they want, fighting them, trying to kill them, or opposing them in other ways.

Often there is one main antagonist opposing the protagonist. That antagonist could be a character working alone or with friends. Harry Potter's main antagonist is the evil wizard Voldemort, who has a number of powerful allies and servants. Harry has other lesser antagonists, too, such as Draco Malfoy, a fellow student who is constantly at odds with Harry.

Sometimes, depending on the story, a particular antagonist will be prominent in part of the story, and a different antagonist will arise in another part. In the early chapters of *Jane Eyre* (Charlotte Brontë), Jane's Aunt Reed is the antagonist. Later, Aunt Reed is out of the picture and Mr. Rochester's murderous wife takes on a sinister presence.

Antagonists aren't necessarily people. Illness, fears, natural disasters, inner flaws, etc., can fulfill the role of antagonist in a story. For example, the main antagonist for Elizabeth Bennett is her own prejudice working against her. For the purposes of this chapter, though, I will refer to antagonists as characters.

The next sections will delve more into creating characters, including protagonists and antagonists.

CHARACTER APPEARANCE

Every time your characters walk onto the page, you want readers to recognize and remember them. This calls for descriptive details. What sets one character apart from the others? A distinctive scar, small eyes, a bizarre hair style?

Some authors imagine their characters with such clarity that they can describe facial features from ears to eyebrows. They can describe bodies down to the shape of a pinky toe. Other authors simply get a feeling for a general outline and then work to fill in the blanks.

Just a few details can bring characters into focus.

When you describe characters in writing, the idea is to give the reader a picture with personality. Descriptive details give information that's either general or specific. Here's a description with only the most general details:

> He was a dark-haired man with blue eyes. He wore glasses. He was dressed in black.

This description isn't complete because the details of dark hair, blue eyes, wearing glasses, and dressed in black, could apply to thousands if not millions of men. There isn't enough to get a feeling for a particular man.

Here's the same guy with a different description that uses more specific details:

> The man's pale blue eyes looked like those of a speared fish. Dark hair fell in limp strands, brushing the smudged lenses of his glasses. His black suit made his skin appear ghostly.

Now we could pick the man out of a crowd. The details woven into his description set a mood. Words like *pale, limp,* and *smudged* give a feeling about this individual man. Comparing his eyes to those of a speared fish and then calling him *ghostly* paints a picture of someone miserable, someone barely able to hang on to life.

Another general description:

> a smiling girl with earrings and a red dress.

Same information with more specifics:

> Ruby stars in the girl's ears matched her red dress and set off her caramel skin. Her smile, brighter than ten chandeliers, shone over the room full of strangers.

Now we get a feeling for the girl's attractive personality. Words like *ruby, stars, caramel,* and *chandeliers* set a whole different mood. This girl shines with life.

A character's style. In fiction, personal style is more important than it is in daily life. You and I can change our appearance drastically without changing who we are. But in fiction, things like clothes and hair matter a lot.

Just a few details can bring characters into focus. Even if you only describe a hairstyle and a hat, you can get a personality to come across on the page.

What sort of assumptions might readers make about a woman with long, dirty hair that has lots of split ends, who is wearing a knit hat that is coming unraveled? They might decide the woman is poor, even homeless. Or she doesn't care much about appearances.

But suppose you change the details, giving your character an elaborate weave braided with gemstones and putting a colorful sun hat on her head. Then she could turn into a model who likes to flaunt her own style.

Gestures are important, too. A girl walking through a hallway chewing her fingernails and then spitting them out will be remembered more than a girl simply walking through a hallway. A man who punches the air with a fist while he talks will make a different impression than a man with his hands in his pockets.

Making an Impression

Try some short character descriptions of your own:
- Write a one-line description of a professional boxer without calling him or her a boxer.
- Write a two-sentence description of a dancer without calling him or her a dancer.
- Write a three-sentence description of a burglar without calling him or her a burglar.

Introducing a new character. When you're ready to put a new character into a story, it works well to slip a description of him or her into a scene where other things are happening. This keeps the description from sounding as if it got dropped on the page in one chunk instead of really being part of the rest of the story.

Here's how one author, David Lubar, introduces a character:

It was in my sixteenth year that faith became an issue. That was the year Sarah moved to town. I met her the first day back at school after the Christmas break. She was walking down the hall, stopping to look at each door, an unfamiliar face, though dressed familiarly enough in jeans and a long-sleeved cotton blouse.

"Lost?" I asked her, figuring she was either a new student or a federal door inspector looking for knob violations.

She gave me an odd smile, as if I'd made a joke, then said, "I can't find room 307."

"Follow me," I said.

That same smile twitched across her lips and spread to her green eyes in the form of a sparkle.

Lubar's character is wearing jeans and a long-sleeved cotton blouse. She has green eyes and a twitchy smile. Because these details are slipped into an ongoing story, they seem more lifelike than if he'd written something like this: *I met Sarah yesterday. She wore jeans and a long-sleeved cotton blouse. She has green eyes and a twitchy smile.*

Building Your Story

Each chapter of *Seize the Story* will have "Building Your Story" writing exercises. They focus on the elements of fiction that go into writing a complete story. If you decide to do all the exercises one by one, by the end of this book you'll have written many scenes and practiced many techniques. Then, if you choose, you can use those pieces of writing as a foundation to finish a story of your own.

The first "Building Your Story" exercise is to pick a character you've created—maybe the one you started getting to know on page 10 or maybe a new one. Whatever character it is, it should be one who matters to you.

Now, using specific details that set a mood and show personality, describe the character.

CHARACTER NAMES

One of the questions I'm most frequently asked is "How do you come up with names for your characters?"

I ask.

Gestures are important, too.

Really. I picture the character sitting across from me and ask, "What's your name?"

Usually the name shows up right there in my mind. (No, I don't hear voices.) But sometimes there's no answer—and when that happens, I open a baby name book and go down the list until I find a name that seems right.

Look for a name that fits the character you have created. Like clothes, names mean more in fiction than they do in real life. A character's name can help show something about the character's nature.

You can always make up names if you like. However, I'd recommend against names that are hard to say or remember. There's no reason to annoy your readers every time they see a complicated name with no vowels or three apostrophes. (Zkllkrn rode off into the sunset. D'nel'bernoth'le went to the store.)

Changing Names

Pick one of your favorite books and open to a random page. Read a few paragraphs aloud, changing the name of the main character. Try it several times with different names. Pick names that seem wrong for the character and then names that seem right.

What do you notice?

When choosing names in your story, be aware of the first letter and try not to repeat the same first letter for main characters. Suze should not go to the archery range with Sam and Serena. Jason should not meet Justin and Jeremy at the mall. Readers start to lose track if character names are easy to mix up.

A related problem is when names in a story all have the same number of syllables. When it comes to syllables, there are plenty of choices in names, and using combinations helps the story have a better rhythm. Vary one-syllable names (Rose, James) with two-syllable names (Mary, Pablo), three-syllable names (Benjamin, Carmella), even four-syllable names (Venezio, Hermione). Variety is key.

Building Your Story

Choose a name for the main character (protagonist) you have created for your story. Write a paragraph about this character, referring to him or her by name.

CONTRASTING CHARACTERS

People often say writers use their imagination most when plotting a story. I disagree. I think we use our imagination most when we create characters. It takes tons of imagination to come up with characters who are unlike ourselves.

We've got to write about people different from us. If every character in a story is just a duplicate of who we are, then what? Without contrasting personalities, things run together. Like a day that never turns to night, it's too much of one thing. It gets boring.

Without antagonists, a story is as blah as a stale marshmallow. Antagonists bring friction between characters. Friction makes things happen.

When you're thinking like a writer, everyone you meet is fascinating, whether you like the person or not—because you're always on the lookout for character traits you haven't seen before. Writers need irritating and disgusting characters just as much as we need those who are lovable and inspiring.

So when you meet that person who gets on your nerves, take lots of notes so you can use them later to create believably obnoxious character traits in fictional people. As you take notes, be specific. What exactly annoys you? Does the person talk nonstop and never listen? Sneeze into her hand and then touch your food? Slack off during group projects? Bully other people? Maybe someone is always smelly. Pinpoint the odor. Is it old shoes and sweaty socks? Mossy teeth? Too much cologne?

Look for a name that fits the character you have created.

Or maybe it's an attitude that gets to you. If so, capture the details. For example, if the person is arrogant and insulting, don't write, "Cody is arrogant and insulting." Write something more specific, like this:

Cody is Mr. "I'm Right." What's so maddening is not just that he thinks he's always right (which, I admit he often is)—it's that he treats me like I'm wrong. If I say anything to him, he doesn't even wait until I finish my sentence before he gets a smirk on his face, tilts his head, scratches under his arms, and makes a monkey call—like I'm on the same intelligence level as a chimpanzee.

Not only will noting the details help you become a better writer, but you'll probably feel better inside once you write down what bothers you. You might even get to the point where you're grateful to all the obnoxious people you've ever met! You can use what you learn from those people to create marvelous antagonists.

Through the Eyes of an Antagonist

Think of a time when you had a fight or an argument with someone you thought was completely wrong. Write down what happened as well as you can remember.

Next, write about the same incident, but this time pretend you're the other person in the "scene"—the person who annoyed you. Use your imagination to view the whole situation the way the antagonist might—feelings, thoughts, actions, everything. If you have trouble, try telling a friend about the fight or argument. Then ask the friend to play you, while you play your antagonist.

Building Your Story

Bring the character you have created—your protagonist—to mind. Now imagine someone who opposes him or her, someone making problems and getting in the way.

You now have an antagonist for your story.

When you have a clear idea of your fictional antagonist, sit down for another interview. Ask: Who are you? Where do you come from? What do you want? Why are you opposing my protagonist? How far would you go to hurt my protagonist? What are your strengths? Do you have any weaknesses? What's your name? What do you look like?

Heroic traits. Your protagonist will probably have at least one heroic trait that inspires you and your readers. He or she will rise above or go beyond big problems, show an exceptional heart or mind, grow deeper or wiser in some way.

So just as you take notes on people you despise, take notes on people you look up to—so you can put wonderful traits into your fictional heroes.

Again, go for details. What precisely do you like? What has the person done? What's outstanding about him or her? Is it kindness? Bravery? Leadership? Ingenuity? Persistence? Humor? (If someone makes you laugh, definitely take notes. Even a dark story can use light moments.) What tone of voice does he/she use? What gestures?

Building Your Story

What character traits do you admire?

Pick a couple of your favorite novels. What do you like about the protagonist? What heroic traits do you notice?

Now bring to mind again the protagonist you have created. Does he or she have some of the same heroic traits? Different ones? What are they? Are any of them strong enough to somehow defeat the antagonist of your story?

CHARACTER MOTIVATION AND STAKES

Characters reveal who they are by the actions they take and the words they speak—and they speak or take action because they care.

Some of the things protagonists might care about deeply:

- Life—their own or the life of someone dear to them
- Love—for family, friends, romantic relationships
- Soul, spirituality
- Health and strength
- Freedom
- Fate of the world
- Honor and reputation

- Skills and knowledge
- Adventure
- Success
- Power
- Money and/or possessions
- Popularity or social status
- Approval
- Escape

The more protagonists care about something, the more they have to lose. The more they have to lose, the more they have at stake.

Different stakes. Stakes are different for two characters even when they're in the same situation. For example, in a story of a hungry wolf chasing a rabbit, the wolf is running for his dinner while the rabbit is running for his life. Obviously, the stakes are higher for the rabbit.

When the stakes go up, so does the tension. When tension rises, a story gets more exciting.

Imagine two young women, Jess and Tiona, who will each play guitar and sing at an open mike in a local coffee shop. Jess wants to be a veterinarian. She plays guitar to unwind and goes to the microphone on a whim. But Tiona has dreamed of a career in music since she was six years old. Someone has just told her that a talent scout from a big record label is sitting in the audience. Jess has nothing at stake except a possible broken string and frightening any dogs who may be listening. Tiona's life dream is at stake.

Robert and Miguel are jumping from rooftop to rooftop, seven stories above the ground. Robert has made the jump every day for the past five months, for fun. But Miguel is deathly afraid of heights and has never done the jump before. Robert isn't worried, but Miguel is terrified he could fall to his death. Different stakes.

Doug asks Ava to go to the prom, and Terrell asks Marisa. Doug and Ava have been a couple for a year and never had a fight. Terrell has been in love with Marisa since third grade but never dared get near her. For Doug, the stakes are low—unless Ava makes a total personality change in twenty-four hours. Terrell has much more at stake.

Raising stakes for characters. When you raise stakes for your characters, you raise stakes for your story. When the stakes are higher, so is the suspense.

If the only thing at stake is an ice cream cone, who cares?—unless your protagonist is a three-year-old.

But what if life hangs in the balance?

Not that every story should come down to life and death, but raising the stakes always helps intensify things. Maybe your main character has squeamishly said *yes* to riding in the cockpit while her friend skydives. Raise the stakes. Make something go wrong with the plane so she's compelled to skydive herself.

The more troubles you give your protagonist, the better. (More about that in other chapters.)

What's at Stake?

To find out what's at stake for characters you create, ask them:
- What do you care about most? Why?
- How would you feel if you lost what you care about?
- What would you do to keep from losing what's important to you?
- What, to you, would be a very bad situation? How would you act if you found yourself in that exact situation—or one even worse?

Goals and wishes. Once you understand what's really at stake for characters, you know what motivates them. Their motivations drive them to have goals and wishes. Their goals and wishes turn into actions.

Their actions move the plot.

Sometimes two characters may take the same action but have different motivations. For example, Gideon and Akeem both play football, but Gideon plays because his goal is to land a football scholarship so he can eventually catch the attention of NFL scouts, while Akeem plays to prove his skills to himself. Both young men want respect, but Gideon is more concerned about his reputation, and Akeem cares more about self-respect.

Molly and Elena get up every morning and jog five miles, but Molly does it because she's on the basketball team and jogging gives her an edge, while Elena runs because it takes away her stress and keeps her weight down. Molly's goal is to be a better basketball player. Elena's goal is to be healthy and feel good.

When the stakes are higher, so is the suspense.

Turning bad days into good stories. We all have days that feel hideously dark and painful. Often, the pain is about other people. Let's face it, occasionally humans can be hard to take—especially when they're being hurtful or infuriating in some way.

But as a writer, you can ask yourself what is motivating people who are doing things you want to scream or cry about. *Why* do they do what they do? If you can understand them, you can create characters with similar motivations—characters readers will love to hate.

I've held a bunch of different jobs, from baking bread to hosting radio shows. I've waited tables, painted houses, and taught anatomy. Those jobs allowed me to meet wildly different people, and they all taught me something about human nature.

When I worked in the corporate world for a while, some of the managers I met were really rigid in their outlook, or so I thought. I tried hard to understand what could possibly motivate them to act the way they did. Then, long after I'd quit the corporate scene, I wrote *The Healer's Keep* and created a whole class of people known as "Dradens" for my book. Dradens always enforce rules, no matter how unreasonable those rules might be.

J.K. Rowling, author of *Harry Potter and the Goblet of Fire*, created Rita Skeeter, an odious reporter who writes lies and prints them as truth. Maybe Rowling created Rita by blending her imagination with a touch of reality after being followed by tabloid reporters. I don't know. Could be. In any case, Rita Skeeter is a delightfully despicable character, a worthy opponent, a nasty antagonist.

As writers, we can use our own misery to write better. We can turn bad days into good stories.

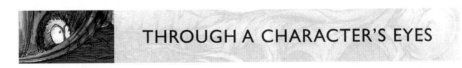

THROUGH A CHARACTER'S EYES

What would happen if you asked seven people who went to the same party to describe what it was like? You would probably hear seven very different versions of what happened. In fact, it might sound as though each person went to a separate party.

As writers, we can use our own misery to write better.

Depending on perspective, there are about ten billion ways to interpret the same event. It's easy to misunderstand what's going on—especially if we're missing a key piece of information.

For instance, when I was teaching an anatomy class for adults, I had a student who sat in the back of the class and never changed her expression. Based on her stone face, I decided she must not think much of the class or the people in it.

Then she came in for some tutoring, and I talked to her. She told me she'd been hit in the face with a hardball. Underneath her skin, her face had been reconstructed with wire mesh. She was lucky to keep her eyesight. Many of her facial muscles didn't even work anymore, so she couldn't change her expression even if she wanted to.

I'd had it all wrong. It turned out she really loved the class. My interpretation was based on what it would mean if *I* had sat in the back of the class never changing expression. But it's a mistake to interpret other people's actions according to what they would mean if they were our own actions. For example, imagine a girl named Mina who is outgoing and loves to talk. When she doesn't talk to someone, it means she doesn't like that person. But her classmate Glenn doesn't talk much because he's shy. He's so shy he can't open his mouth around Mina because he has a crush on her. Mina assumes Glenn's silence means the same thing to him that it would mean to her. She thinks he doesn't like her, while the truth is quite the opposite.

We all share the same world, but we never know how others will see things, hear things, and put things together in their minds.

We don't know, but we can imagine.

Writing as someone else. When you look at the world through the eyes and ears of other people—whether they're real or imaginary—it helps with the process of creating realistic characters. No matter where you are, you can imagine how different people would experience the same place.

Let's say I'm at the beach, listening to the shrieking gulls. As I sit on my black and yellow towel with the heat baking my skin, I begin to imagine what other people might say about this same beach.

I start with a good friend, someone I know well. I can easily imagine myself as him because I'm familiar with his personality. I think about the way he would hear the waves, smell the air, and see the intense sunlight.

Then I begin writing. The "I" viewpoint is his, imagined by me:

Every time I see a wave roll out to sea it carries another worry away. The sky's so big and the sand's so wide, I can actually see the curve of the horizon, which makes me realize my problems aren't as big as I thought they were.

Who knows if what I'm imagining is really the way my friend would feel and think? But I still like pretending to have his perspective.

Next, I notice an old woman reclining in a chair farther down the beach. She seems tired and sick. Her hands tremble. I ask myself what it would be like to be so feeble. Imagining myself as her, I write:

The sound of the surf is soothing, but it doesn't quite drown out my pain. Good thing I wore my thick sunglasses, because the sun would stab my eyes if I didn't have their protection. Still, it's beautiful here. I wish I could go back in time and run into the waves, feel the water rushing past, smell the brine close to my nose. But I can't. Not today, not ever again.

Same place but a very different perspective.

Then I see a teenage boy twenty yards away, sitting alone and staring morosely at the ocean. I imagine he's just gone through breaking up with a girlfriend. As him, I write:

I know why they brought me to the beach. They think it's going to make me quit thinking about the breakup. It's not going to work. So what if the waves smash in and out? I don't care if the water has beaten mountains of rock into grains of sand. Doesn't matter to me. The air smells like dead fish.

Wherever you go, your imagination goes with you. Like a muscle, the more you use it, the stronger it gets. When you imagine what other people are going through—even strangers—you increase your imaginative powers. Then it becomes easier to create characters that seem realistic.

Looking at the world through the eyes and ears of other people will help you create realistic characters.

Picking a **Perspective**

Looking at the world through the eyes and ears of people who aren't you really helps strengthen your imagination for character creation. In this exercise, you can pick several possible perspectives from a list to get started. (You can find many more perspectives in your daily life.)

Possible perspectives:
- of a good friend
- of someone you admire
- of someone you dislike
- of someone wise
- of someone younger than you
- of someone old and sick
- of someone injured or handicapped
- of an employee
- of a boss
- of someone broken-hearted
- of a musician/artist/actor
- of an immigrant with different ancestry from yours
- of someone who lives to play sports
- of a character from a fairy tale

Pick three perspectives from the list above, and imagine how each of those characters would experience one of the following scenes:
- a day at the beach
- a car crash in front of his or her home
- a five-star restaurant
- a small party of close friends
- a huge concert
- a store robbery
- a UFO sighting
- a relationship breaking up
- boarding an airplane
- any other incident you like

Now write about the scene from each of the perspectives you have chosen.

Building Your Story

Imagine an important event in the life of your protagonist, something hard to live through, something that had a big impact. Write about what happened from the protagonist's perspective. Include feelings, thoughts, reactions, interpretations.

Then imagine that your antagonist was at the same event but interpreted everything differently and totally misunderstood how the protagonist reacted.

Write about what happened from the antagonist's perspective.

PRIMARY AND SECONDARY CHARACTERS

Primary characters, whether protagonists or antagonists, are of first importance. The story is all about *them.*

Secondary characters have lives too, but they don't get as much face time and their actions are important only because of how they affect a primary character. (The difference between primary and secondary characters is similar to the difference between the "Best Actor" and "Best Supporting Actor" categories at awards shows for movies.)

Sometimes secondary characters show up in only one or two scenes in your story. Maybe they're trash collectors or dinner servers, mail carriers or random Martians—people who don't have a big part in the overall story but still have a vital piece of information for the protagonist.

And sometimes secondary characters are involved in lots of pivotal scenes. They could be good friends with the protagonist, a love interest or mentor, or a dangerous henchman allied with an antagonist.

Many writers end up creating secondary characters with such strong personalities that they start to take over the story. These characters suddenly become more interesting than the protagonist—and more fun. (This happens sometimes in movies and TV shows too, when someone with a secondary part outshines the lead role and steals the show.)

If you find yourself looking forward to writing about a secondary character far more than your protagonist, stop and look at what's going on. When it happens to me, I ask myself why my secondary character is shining brighter and brighter. Is the secondary character really the protagonist? Should I start over completely? What have I done?

When a secondary character steals the show in my work, it usually means I've cut myself off from my protagonist and am starting to get blocked about the story I'm writing. I know I need to turn the light higher on the main character to get past the block. It might work differently for you, though, so keep asking yourself questions until you know what needs to be done on behalf of your story.

One thing I never do is turn down the light on the secondary character so that a protagonist who has become dull will look better. Doing that means I have *two* boring characters instead of one.

Secondary characters can really make or break a story, so go ahead and give them plenty of attention. Interview them. Describe them and name them with as much care as if they are primary characters.

A look at a secondary character. In the fairy tale "Cinderella," Cinderella is a primary character. But perhaps the secondary characters in that story have more going on than we usually imagine.

An interesting exercise asks writers to retell a scene from a well-known fairy tale from the perspective of one of the secondary characters. In response to the exercise, author Todd Mitchell said, "The scene I chose was the moment in 'Cinderella' (the Brothers Grimm version—which is deliciously bloody) when one of Cinderella's stepsisters is persuaded by her mom to cut off her toes to make her foot fit in the shoe Cinderella left behind at the ball. In writing this scene, I surprised myself by discovering that the so-called 'ugly stepsister' is actually a far more sympathetic and interesting character than I'd thought."

Here is Mitchell's scene, written from the perspective of Cinderella's stepsister:

> When Mom asked me to cut off my toes, I wasn't very surprised.
>
> "I only want what's best for you," she said, dragging a hair across the edge of the butcher's knife. The blade, newly sharpened, split the hair in half. "Life is full of suffering," she said. "I pluck my eyebrows every morning. This will only hurt for a moment, and then we'll be set for life."

Secondary characters can really make or break a story.

She handed the butcher's knife to me and indicated the chopping block that she'd placed an old curtain under to keep the blood from staining the floor.

"Go on then," she said, glancing nervously at the door to the living room where the prince was waiting. "And don't scream. If he hears you, he might suspect something."

She crossed her arms, and turned her back to me.

So why did I do it?

It wasn't to please her, that's for certain. And it wasn't to marry the prince, either. For months, I'd been sneaking out to meet Robert, my true love, in the woods. That oaf of a prince appealed to me about as much as a hangnail. But what other way did I have to break free from my mother? From my life?

I clenched my jaw and raised the butcher's knife.

I had to change myself. I had to bleed.

Building Your Story

Bring to mind either a protagonist or an antagonist from the story you are creating. Now imagine a secondary character related to the protagonist or antagonist, a character who will play an ongoing role in your story, or someone with a walk-on part.

Interview the character. Describe him or her in detail, and come up with a name.

REAL LIFE VS. FICTION

People can be optimistic, despairing, generous, stingy, perceptive, knowledgeable, clueless, loving, lonely, impulsive, cautious, lost, driven, dreamy, practical, kind, cruel, strong, wounded, devout, scientifically-minded, flighty, grounded, nerdy, stylish, self-confident, timid, courageous, cowardly…you name it.

In daily life, people often fluctuate from one character trait to another. One minute they're considerate, the next minute mean. One minute ready for fun, the next full of gloom and doom. One minute inspired, the next listless and drained.

But fictional characters are more consistent. They demonstrate certain traits without fail, traits by which we get to know them.

If you were to list character traits for your friends, you'd probably list dozens of traits for each friend. But try listing traits for people in books or movies. You'll find far fewer per character. There's a reason for that. If fictional characters had dozens of traits each, the characters would be less distinct. They would start over-lapping in the reader's mind.

Even five significant traits would be a lot for a primary character in a story. And secondary characters sometimes have only one trait, such as loyalty, geeki-ness, or an ability to be funny.

Good news: You can create well-rounded characters by playing up just a few traits in each one.

Looking at Character Traits

Focus on a favorite book or movie. Pick a primary character and a second-ary character. Then list character traits for each. How many do you find in the primary character? How many in the secondary character?

COMMON PROBLEMS IN CHARACTERIZATION

Problems often come up for new writers creating characters. Here are four of the most common.

Characters fall out of character. A city girl who fears horses but then casually jumps on a wild mustang and goes for a nice ride has fallen out of character. So has a man who has always loved hunting his own food in the wilderness and then moves to a city apartment and eats nothing but deli take-out.

Both character transformations are possible and enjoyable—*if* they're ex-plained during the course of a story. But they can't come out of the blue. Major changes require powerful motivation, and writers must show how and why the character is changing. If a five-foot-tall girl suddenly beats the six-foot-tall class bully in a physical fight, it won't make any sense unless the writer has taken care to show the girl attending aikido classes every night for a year, or something like that. It isn't enough to simply announce that the girl went to aikido classes. Scenes about aikido are necessary. How did the girl feel when she learned how to fall without getting hurt? What about the first time she threw someone bigger than herself?

Characters have no flaws. We all make mistakes, and it's hard to relate to characters who don't. There's got to be something they fail to consider or something they do that has dire consequences.

In my first book, Landen (the male protagonist) underestimates both his enemy, Vesputo (the male antagonist), and the woman he loves, Torina (female protagonist). In turn, Torina allows fear and anger arising from the past to take over her life for a while. These are serious flaws, and they are necessary. Without them, the book would be about as exciting as a warm bottle of pop without the fizz.

Think over books and movies you have enjoyed. What flaws are present in the characters? How do those flaws make the action more interesting?

Just as we all make mistakes, we all have quirks. A small weakness helps make a character unforgettable. Maybe a model has dirty fingernails or keeps losing her phone. Maybe a basketball star can't do free throws, and his shoelaces keep coming undone. Maybe an art major turns out to be color blind and always wears mismatched socks.

Characters are taken straight from real-life people. If a character has the same mannerisms, ideas, problems, and personality of someone you actually know, you haven't created a character. You have simply duplicated someone.

If other people can recognize the person from what you've written, and you've made that person look bad, you've done something illegal. Everyone (except a celebrity) is entitled to privacy about his or her life.

Although it's important to observe and record real people, be sure you've mixed and matched individual traits in your imaginary characters.

Characters are stereotypes. When characters have nothing unique about them, they drag your story down.

Imagine a police officer. He's dressed in a normal uniform. "This is a crime scene," he says. "Please move back."

We've seen this character a hundred times before in books, movies, and TV shows. There is nothing interesting about him.

But if we alter the stereotype, the character is more intriguing, as in the following example:

> The pants on her police uniform had neat stitching, but anyone could tell they'd been hemmed up. Short legs. Very short. Regulation size gun, though, and her voice matched her weapon. "Crime," she said. "Scene." Her glare intensified when a man took a step forward. "Back. We don't allow civilians inside the perimeter."

Now the character is more original. She could turn out to be either a primary or secondary character. Either way, she is more interesting than the stereotype.

CHARACTERS WHO MATTER TO YOU

You might be someone who creates characters by letting them form in your unconscious mind to the point where they wake you up from a sound sleep and breathe down your neck.

Or you might patiently build them in a conscious way, trait by trait, until they stand whole and complete.

You might do something in between, or you might do something I've never heard of doing.

But whether you're creating kings or dragons, linebackers or androids, ducklings or assorted monsters, mechanics, criminals, eagles, or astronauts—write about characters who matter to you.

It makes all the difference. It really does.

Fictional characters have to remain in character until something happens to change them.

BEGINNINGS

CHAPTER THREE

BEGINNINGS

**The last thing one discovers in composing
a work is what to put first.**
— Blaise Pascal

**Draw your chair up close to the edge of
the precipice and I'll tell you a story.**
— F. Scott Fitzgerald

In order to really start writing your story, you have to begin. How's that for profound and glorious advice?

And as you bravely set out to write, you might wonder if you need an outline before starting your first chapter.

To outline or not to outline, that is the question—and everyone seems to have an opinion about it. Those opinions often land on opposite sides.

I've heard many versions of this: "You must outline! If you don't, you have no idea where you're going. You'll write yourself into a dead end and have to start over. Writers who don't outline are fooling themselves."

And I've heard just as many versions of the opposite view: "Fiction writers create stories as they go along. Outlining is a waste of time and interferes with creativity. Besides, even if you get an outline together, the story will change completely once you get started."

Maybe both opinions keep coming up because they're both true. They're both true because different writers work in different ways.

Some people outline. Some don't. Some scribble a kind of writer's sketch— disorganized notes about scenes that come to mind. There's no formula.

I've tried several times to outline stories in advance, but outlining doesn't work for me. Apparently my unconscious mind just doesn't want my conscious fingers to touch the story too soon. My characters refuse to tell me what's next unless I'm writing actual scenes, not notes about scenes. Once the story is already written, then I can come up with an outline. Not before.

But my writing style might not match yours at all. You might be more like Hilari Bell, one of the authors interviewed at the end of this book. She outlines her novels in advance, and that works very well for her. There are plenty of other writers who can't imagine beginning a story without knowing where it's going.

The important question is: What will actually work for *you?*

If outlining suits you, go ahead. Enjoy it. I honestly envy you. When you wonder what in the world comes next in your story, your outline will give you a clue.

But if you can't outline, don't worry. You're not alone. Like many other writers, I would end my career in a pit of despair if I had to outline in advance.

Starting points. Two thousand three hundred fifty years ago, a Greek man named Aristotle advised playwrights to begin their stories *in media res,* which means in the middle of the action. Aristotle's advice was so good it's still relevant today.

In other words, the best place to start is when things are happening.

The writer Kurt Vonnegut said, "Begin as close to the end as possible"—his way of saying *in media res.*

My advice: Begin with something that throws the lives of your characters into chaos and disaster.

Well, maybe you don't have to start with instant misery. You can show peace and happiness to make it clear the characters have something to lose—right before you drastically shake up their lives. But don't linger on the happy stuff.

Think of your favorite books and movies. What happens to the characters near the beginning? In what way and how fast are their lives turned upside down? Stories old and new show what is meant by *in media res.*

Early in the ancient story of *Beowulf,* a monster named Grendel is going on nightly rampages, terrorizing and killing the people of Denmark.

At the beginning of *Hope Was Here,* by Joan Bauer, we learn that Hope Yancey's mother deserted her at birth, leaving her to be raised by her aunt. The aunt works very hard, but then her life savings are stolen by her business partner, and she and Hope must leave their beloved New York City for a small town in Wisconsin.

In the beginning of my book *The Seer and the Sword,* Prince Landen loses his father, his kingdom, his sword, and his freedom. In *The Healer's Keep,* Maeve is

The best place to start is when things are happening.

sold to the fearsome Lord Morlen and discovers her mother is dying. Early in *The Light of the Oracle*, Bryn witnesses the death of the only person who understands her. She leaves home and finds out the people she's traveling with have tried to kill another young woman.

You can go all the way back to "The Three Little Pigs." In every story, it isn't long before a version of the Big Bad Wolf appears, huffing and puffing, making a scene.

Scenes. I'll be recommending that you write a scene for the next "Building Your Story" exercise, so this seems like a good place to define what a scene *is*.

A scene is a part of the story with a specific focus.

Scenes can be short or long depending on the focus. They usually take place in one location, though there are exceptions.

Here are descriptions of two different scenes from one book, *Under a War-Torn Sky,* by L. M. Elliott. The protagonist is Henry, a young fighter pilot in World War II.

- In one scene, Henry floats toward earth supported by his escape parachute after his plane has been shot down. A German fighter plane flies straight at him, shooting holes in his parachute. Out of his mind with grief and anger, Henry uses his pistol to try shooting the zooming plane. He wastes all his ammunition and then throws the gun itself like a missile, a useless gesture. His parachute ruined, he sees the ground rushing toward him.

  The focus of this scene is Henry's fall to earth and his helplessness in the face of the Nazi war machine.

- In another scene, Henry is invited to dinner at a cottage in war-torn France. The focus of this scene is peace: savory smells, flowers, handcrocheted curtains, spotless copper pots. The warmth and food remind Henry of home and what he's fighting for. Everything is in contrast to the world of war.

Writing scenes. Scenes, like stories, have beginnings, middles, and ends. The beginning sets the tone. The middle brings action. The end is quick.

When you first write a scene, let it gush like water through a big pipe. Don't worry about the structure. Whatever occurs to you, write it down. But once you've finished, go back and ask yourself about the focus. Take out anything that doesn't fit.

For example, if Henry had been able to injure a German warplane with a pistol, the fearsome aspect of the Nazis would have been diminished. And if the French kitchen where he's invited to dinner had been grimy and cold, it wouldn't have furnished a poignant contrast to war.

Building Your Story

Imagine a scene for your story where the protagonist's life is seriously disrupted. Write that scene, getting things moving, shaking things up, and bringing on trouble.

SETTING

CHAPTER FOUR

SETTING

The world is but a canvas to the imagination.
— Henry David Thoreau

If you've ever been involved in a play, you know how much thought and effort goes into building sets. From the painted backdrop to the arrangement of furniture and props, the setting around characters on stage enhances the drama.

Settings are just as important in written fiction, and you don't have the limits of a stage production. You can put your characters into any setting you like and then change it to suit the action of your story.

In fiction, setting always has three components: place, time, and mood. The characters are *somewhere*. They are in that place at a particular *time*. Their surroundings also have an atmosphere, or *mood*. All of this sets the tone for what happens.

Place, time, and mood. Imagine yourself touring Carlsbad Caverns, one of the biggest caves in the world. The air is musty, and burly stalactites and stalagmites are staring you down.

Now imagine standing on top of the Empire State Building in New York City on a summer day. A haze of pollution smudges the view.

Next, imagine lounging next to basking beach bums and tourists in Miami. Colorful towels and oiled-up bodies carpet the sand.

With each change in place, the mood changes, too. If you write a story with a setting of Carlsbad Caverns, it will probably be quite different from a story with a setting on the Empire State Building or a setting at Miami Beach.

Going back to Carlsbad Caverns, imagine you're there at a time before anyone else has discovered the cave, a time when well-lit guided tours have never been heard of and all you've got is a candle for light—a candle with a dying flame that throws flickering shadows into what seems to be endless darkness.

The change in time period brings about a change in atmosphere. Now the stories you might imagine with Carlsbad Caverns as a setting will be different than they would be in contemporary times.

Envision the Empire State Building in the future when it's considered a rather small skyscraper. Hovercraft buzz past. Air pollution has been solved, so the air is pure and clear. How does this change affect the story action that might occur?

Mood elements. By shifting various elements of setting, we can create more flavors of mood. Imagine a couple warming themselves beside a campfire in a forest during a drought in Colorado. The fire hazard is high, which sets a mood of anxiety and risk. But a hearth fire inside a lodge during a gentle rain would set a serene, peaceful mood instead.

When describing a setting, you're describing a mood as much as you're describing the place itself. It all comes down to how you want your readers to feel. Therefore you'd choose different words to describe the campfire in the drought-ridden forest than you would to describe the hearth fire in the lodge. To describe the campfire, you might say: *The fire crackled menacingly, throwing out angry sparks.* To set a different mood with the hearth fire, you might say: *The smiling flames rose and fell like graceful dancers.*

When a setting is described without a mood, the description may be accurate but rather lifeless. For example: *The fire was inside a pit surrounded by stones. The flames were approximately two feet at their highest, but sparks frequently flew past the perimeter of the pit.*

Setting a Mood

Decide on a specific mood you want for a scene in a story. Describe the setting using words that show mood.

 ## WRITING WHAT YOU KNOW

Before we go farther into how to work with setting, let's veer into another subject for a moment.

Suspension of disbelief is a rather convoluted term that means your readers must be able to believe in your story even though they know it isn't true. In other words, they must be willing to accept what is happening in the world of the story and let themselves be drawn into it as it unfolds—by suspending a sense of disbelief. (Don't ask me who came up with the term *suspension of disbelief*. All I can tell you is we writers are probably stuck with it, so it's worth memorizing.)

Suspension of disbelief will likely fail—meaning the reader won't be quite able to believe what is going on in the story—if a character is struck by lightning and just keeps walking, or eats two hundred hotdogs in an hour without getting violently sick, or becomes a black belt in karate in two months. Readers know better, so they will stop believing in the story.

Anyway, if you've taken writing classes, you've probably heard the saying "Write what you know." The reason for this advice is that realistic details make a story more believable. If you're a swimmer, you know swimming, so you can write believably about it. If you're a gardener, you know plants, so you can easily write scenes with plants in them. If you have a phobia about spiders, you can communicate it on the page without doing extra research. You're writing about what you already know.

And one of the best ways to get a reader to believe in your story is by adding realistic, convincing details to a setting. To find those details, practice taking notes wherever you go. That way, you really get to know the places you've been.

The art of taking notes. When you're in motion, you can't actually write things down, but you can take mental notes, noticing everything around you, and writing them later.

When you take notes, focus on all five of the basic physical senses.

What are the sights? Colors, patterns, images, movement? What's the quality of the light—is it smoky, hazy, bright, shadowed, etc.? What's the quality of the space—open and spacious or airless and enclosed?

What are the sounds? Are they musical or harsh to your ears? Quiet, loud, muted, roaring, swishing, dripping?

Practice taking notes wherever you go.

What are the smells? Fragrant, piercing, light, fresh, heavy, clinging? Minty, rotten, musky?

What tastes are available? Sweet, salty, pungent, bitter, acrid, sour, delicious?

What does the place feel like to the touch? Rough, smooth, soft, hard, grainy, warm, cold?

Also take note of the emotions you feel when you're in different places, or the emotions you notice in others. Sad, happy, thrilled, bored, hopeful, angry, amazed…all of these feelings are part of the mood, and the mood is part of the setting.

Let's say someone named Aurora ends up on vacation somewhere in the desert and doesn't enjoy anything about it. Her throat is parched, the heat throbs in her brain until she can barely think, and the reptiles freak her out. Also, there's nothing to do. But Aurora wants to be a writer, so she takes notes, even though she's not enjoying herself. Maybe her notes will be brief:

> sun too bright, hurts my eyes
> deathly quiet
> parched throat, gritty mouth, chapped lips, throbbing head
> air smells like burned dust, nothing growing but prickles

Or she might write more:

> Today my throat is so dry, when I talk it sounds like a metal spoon scraping against a rock. My lips look like they're becoming reptile skin, shedding ugly brown flakes. Nothing grows here, unless you count weird, twisty, prickled plants. Snakes slither around and flick their tongues, while lizards dart back and forth like they're going out of their tiny little minds.

But let's say someone named Wayne goes to the desert and loves being there. His notes will be different. If he is brief:

> sunsets all across the sky
> zipping lizards
> quiet and peaceful
> smells clean and ancient

If he writes in more detail:

> I like to look out over the miles of sand and see things I've never seen at home—leaning towers of rock, spiky cacti, racing lizards. The sun never tires. I'm storing up heat to last through the next cold winter. The air smells like wisdom, full of peace.

Same place, different description. With the different description, a different mood is set for the reader.

Everything you do. Everything you do also has the potential to be woven into a story setting.

While playing basketball, you might notice how the gym reverberates when the ball is dribbled. You might make a mental note of the expressions on the faces of the other players, the pounding rush of feet up and down the court, the sensation you feel when the ball leaves your hand and you already know it's going to bounce off the rim.

If you play a musical instrument—maybe the French horn—you record how it feels to carry the horn around, to shine the bell, to stuff music into the case. You remember the metallic taste of the mouthpiece. You watch the band director and how she moves when waving her baton, how she taps her podium to stop the music, how she glares at the section that comes in late.

On my first visit to Colorado from Oregon, I arrived by bicycle—a journey of about 1,200 miles. Riding (and sometimes walking my bike) across forests, deserts, and three mountain ranges taught me a lot about terrain. I remember sitting on a mossy boulder next to a waterfall in western Oregon during a time when rain had been falling steadily for almost a week. Then there were days spent under the grilling sun in the deserts. I had to slather myself with zinc oxide to avoid getting toasted beyond human recognition. In the Rocky Mountains, it snowed during the night, turning my sleeping bag into a freezing sponge.

Now, when I write about a character wading an icy stream or half dying in the desert, I draw from experience to add details that make the scene real.

Imagination plus reality. Imagination plus reality equals a convincing setting.

Author Laura Resau spent two years in the mountainous Mixtec region of Oaxaca, Mexico. She carried a notebook everywhere, recording details of the culture and people. Filtering her experiences through her imagination, she wrote captivating books like *What the Moon Saw* and *Red Glass.*

In the river scene of Todd Mitchell's book *The Traitor King*, the protagonist rides the rapids in the company of pixies and a brownie. The river is like those found on Earth, but the pixies and brownies are imaginary. Because the river is so convincing, the imaginary beings seem more real. The river details are convincing because of Mitchell's real-life kayaking experience—he describes roaring water as only someone who's been scrambled around in a kayak can do.

I used to work as a cook in a large kitchen. The following scene is part of a fantasy I wrote, but the concrete details come from those days I spent cooking:

> Dak tested the croutons with a quick nip of his fingers. Crisp. He grabbed the bowl, sprinkling crumbs into simmering butter, stirring gently before adding chopped onions and sage. Beside him, Nan darted about like a bird, broken-winged yet fearless.
>
> Dak heard a racket outside the kitchen; a great stamping of booted feet, and a loud voice barking orders. Nan dropped the pan she was greasing, and her skin turned as white as the flour streaking her hair. Even her lips lost color.
>
> "Hide," she said, rasping as if someone squeezed her windpipe.
>
> With a shaking hand she pushed Dak toward the cupboard beneath the counter. Struggling with the door, she urged him through it. As Dak squeezed in among the barrels of flour, sugar and salt, he barely fit, and realized with sudden dread that there was room for only one.

I chose a big kitchen as the setting for an attack because I felt it would enhance the feeling of fear and chaos in the scene. A kitchen is normally a place of nourishment, warmth, and safety, so when people are attacked there, it's somehow worse than on the street or under a bridge.

There are thousands upon thousands of settings available, and you get to choose the one you want—the one that will enhance the story you're telling.

Concrete and Convincing Details

The main focus of the scene on p. 44 isn't cooking, but the details about cooking make the scene believable.

Think about something you know well or something you've often done. It could be as simple as taking out the garbage or checking books out of the library. What are the little details of the situation you chose? What do you notice with your five senses?

Make up a character and put that character into a similar setting. Add convincing details as you write about it.

 ## WRITING WHAT YOU DON'T KNOW

Can we write about places we've never been and things we've never done? Of course. We can, we should, and we will. If we only write what we know, imagination doesn't have much scope.

So what do you do when your story leads you into a setting that's completely strange to you?

A little research pays off. Otherwise you might end up writing about characters who hike for two weeks in the spring in Oregon without seeing a drop of rain—or something just as unlikely.

I wrote a scene in *The Healer's Keep* about the wreck of a ship carrying wine bottles. In my scene, the bottles floated on the ocean like corks. I gave the sixty-third draft of the manuscript to my engineer father, and he pointed out that wine bottles would sink, not float. I hadn't checked my facts before writing. Needless to say, I had to rewrite the scene. (Draft number sixty-four.)

If I had left the bobbing wine bottles to drift on the surface of the ocean in my novel, readers who knew better would find that unforgivable. Disbelief would no longer be suspended—it would crash, along with the story.

If you're not sure about something, find out. How long does it take to fire a piece of pottery? To become a black belt? To plow up a field of corn? What's the germination time for bamboo? Will global warming lead to floods or drought in

Imagination plus reality equals a convincing setting.

the part of the world where you've put your characters? What do animals do during a blizzard?

Some writers get their information off the Internet, carefully double-checking all their sources. Others prefer talking to someone who's an expert. For example, when author Laura Resau wanted to know what would happen to a child found wandering alone after an illegal border crossing, she called Border Patrol to find out.

Building Your Story

When you're ready to write an action scene in your story, ask yourself what setting will enhance that scene the most. What time, place, and mood do you want?

Try out different settings in your mind. Which works best?

Write your scene, describing details to set the mood.

COMMON PROBLEMS WITH DESCRIBING SETTING

New writers are prone to making a number of common mistakes when describing setting. Here are some common problems with description:

Description is too wordy. Long, poetic descriptions are known as "purple prose." Here's an example:

Gloria gazed out toward the shimmering mountain peak, where snow caught the brilliant sunshine and reflected it back in a gleaming haze of intense white. The mountain touched the sky like a proud sail against blue water. As she watched, the golden sun edged toward the stark horizon, and the sky began to darken just a little. Soon, glowing streamers of orange light formed the clouds into a bower of heavenly fire. Then red appeared, and hints of magenta and violet converged into a stupendous display of breathtaking beauty.

If we only write what we know, imagination doesn't have much scope.

Adjectives have their place, but too many will weigh a story down like cement blocks tied to the feet of a drowning man.

A better description of a sunset, one that wouldn't interfere with the story itself, might be something like this:

> Gloria looked toward the gleaming peak. As she watched, the sun dropped, leaving a dark red sky.

As writers, we have an affection for words, phrases, and paragraphs. That's as it should be, but not everyone shares that affection. Long descriptions of oceans, sunsets, and mountain peaks aren't that interesting to most readers, who would rather get on with the action. So if you want to string adjectives like pearls, there's no reason you can't—while you're freewriting.

Instead of drawing out descriptions of scenery for poetic effect, weave short descriptions into action and dialogue, as author Laura Resau does in the excerpt below. There are plenty of details, but she never gets long-winded. Each detail supports the story.

> Back at the house, Dika and Abuelita and the aunts and cousins sat inside the yellow glow of the smoky kitchen, sipping lemongrass tea and eating pastries. I snuck past them and slipped into the bedroom.
>
> It was still inside, the darkness a ghostly blue. No one was there except for Na'nu, who lay on the floor next to the mattress, her hair fanned out like ancient cobwebs. She didn't seem to notice me open my backpack and take out a tiny hair pin. I tiptoed behind the sheet-curtain that divided the men's and women's sections of the room.
>
> I found Ángel's backpack wedged in the corner next to some crates of clothes. Quietly, I unzipped it and moved my hand around. And yes, there it was, his mysterious box, carefully wrapped in a T-shirt. I held the box in my lap, running my fingers over the carved leaves the way Ángel always did. I shook it gently and heard a thunk. It sounded like a stack of papers hitting the sides. A treasure map and notes on its location? Or letters from his mother that she'd secretly sent over the years, from where, maybe, she lived in hiding?
>
> I took a deep breath. I bent the hair pin open, slipped it inside the keyhole and wiggled it.
>
> And then the sheet-curtain rustled.

Adjectives have their place, but too many will weigh a story down.

Purple Prose on Purpose

Sometimes you can learn a lot by doing the opposite of what you should do. Look over Resau's scene, above, and list the descriptive details. Then rewrite the scene, burdening it with excessive description. At what point does the story get lost?

Description doesn't tell readers *where* they are. This problem is the opposite of purple prose. When writers don't add enough description, readers are left wondering where the characters are. Here's an example of too little description:

> Will opened the door to Tamika. They went downstairs. Will showed her the place where he kept his journal.

Without any details, the reader doesn't have a way to experience the characters or their surroundings. Where is "downstairs?" A basement? A crawlspace? What does the journal look like? What's going on?

Description doesn't tell readers *when* they are. We all like to place ourselves in time as well as space. Let your readers know the age of your characters and the era surrounding them. Be clear about time of day and season of year.

Do you want readers to know it's winter? Add a dash of snow and a shiver despite a warm coat. Summer? Mention that your hero nearly expired of heat exhaustion before he could get the car window open.

Description sets the wrong mood. Sometimes writers emphasize details that don't work with a story. If a character is afraid in the wilderness, a description of cheerfully whistling birds would throw off the mood. It would be better to cast a scene full of sinister rustling sounds.

Description uses only one of the five senses. Some authors are so visual they describe everything in terms of what is seen. Others focus on dialogue and tone of voice. But remember, tastes, scents, and touch can add a lot to a setting.

Laura Resau's example on page 47 integrates sight, sound, and touch. There's even a hint of taste in the mention of "lemongrass tea" and a smidgen of smell in the "smoky kitchen."

As you write more, you'll learn which sense you tend to favor. Personally, I often forget about smells and have to remind myself to add a dab of scent to my writing.

The trick is to combine sense impressions without overdoing it. Too much smell will make your story stink. Too much taste will make readers want to spit. The story must always come first.

Using All Five Senses

Find a scene you have already written. It might be from the story you are building, or it might be from something entirely different.

Look at the scene and notice which sense you seem to prefer. Then rewrite the scene, adding details from different senses. If you've written plenty for a reader to hear but nothing to see, put in visual details. Then throw in some sensual words like *velvety* or *bumpy*. And perhaps a whiff of chocolate cookie or fishy fumes.

Building Your Story

Check the setting you wrote from the exercise on page 46. Have you included details about time as well as place?

Descriptions that vividly communicate an atmosphere enhance any drama—whether on a stage, in a movie, or in a book. If actors had to play their parts against a blank backdrop on a stage with no furnishings, or with only a blank screen behind them in a movie, their performances wouldn't have the same chance to grip the hearts and minds of those who are watching. The books we enjoy also have settings, powerful parts of the story that help draw us in.

Putting characters into living settings with the right time, place, and mood is a launching device to drive the story into the imagination of readers.

Let your readers know the age of your characters and the era surrounding them.

THE HEART OF A WRITER

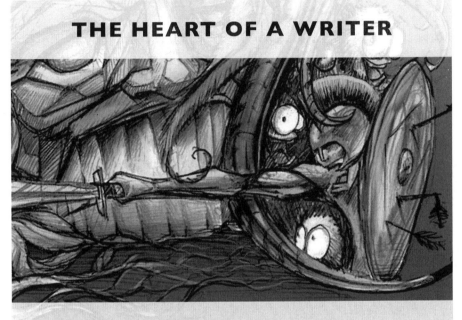

CHAPTER FIVE

THE HEART OF A WRITER

**Better to write for yourself and have no public,
than to write for the public and have no self.**
— Cyril Connolly

There's a powerful "you" factor in writing. It's why you want to write in the first place, and what you bring to a story. There's no one else just like you. And when you put yourself into your writing, you add an ingredient more precious than any technique could possibly deliver.

Voice. Remember the first book that reached across the pages to grip you so tightly the story wouldn't let go until you finished it? And then the same thing happened again, with another book written in a different style by a different author.

Many authors, many voices. We wouldn't all want to sound the same. If we did, the magic would be lost—the spark of unique expression that animates our stories would go out.

Author voices. One of the reasons I've put examples of other writers in this book is because they write differently from each other and differently from me. That's voice.

The way authors show their voices is through their writing style—their choice of words combined with the rhythm and flow of their sentences. One of the easiest ways to show the connection between voice and style is by looking at examples from individual authors and then rewriting them to try to take away the voice.

First, let's look at a piece of writing by author Denise Vega, just as she wrote it:

> If anyone had told me I'd be babysitting my boyfriend's boozed up mother on prom night while he was out with another girl, I would have personally tightened up her straightjacket before waving good-bye to her as she left for the loony bin.
>
> But here I was at Josh's house in my stunning "no one will see it now" three hundred dollar Jessica McClintock dress, making sure Blotto Mama was still breathing.
>
> She was, so I ordered a pizza. Even saints get hungry.

Now the same content, but rewritten in a bland style and removing the humor and flair:

> I would have been upset if anyone had told me that on prom night I'd be watching over my boyfriend's mother after she'd had too much to drink. Josh went to the prom with another girl, leaving me to wear my new dress with no one to see it.
>
> Josh's mother passed out. I checked to see if she was okay, and then I ordered a pizza because I was hungry.

What happens to Vega's voice?

Here are two more examples written in different voices and styles. This one is from author David Lubar:

> It's ironic that Mom named me Faith, since I don't seem to have any. Too bad she didn't name me Excess Fat. I'd certainly love cruising through life without any of that. Mom was going to church big time when I was born, and even when my sister Hope was born. That's how we got such virtuous names. But she stopped pretty soon after that. Good thing. I doubt my little brother would have liked being named Charity, or whatever the masculine version is. Charade? No way. Jasper definitely suits him better.
>
> Anyhow, except for a couple of weddings and a bar mitzvah, and one desperate dash into Our Lady of Mercy to use the bathroom last June,

I'd almost never found myself in a church, synagogue, temple, cathedral, mosque, or shrine during the first fifteen years of my life.

This one is from author James Van Pelt:

> Clarence envisioned the virus like a horrible mold. Its name sounded like a mold, poliomyelitis. The doctors put his useless legs in casts. Itching during the day was intolerable, but Clarence could force a pencil, or a ruler, or a straightened coat hanger only so far under the plaster. Maybe the virus really resembled a mold, growing out of sight in the cast's moist darkness. If the casts came off now, would his legs look human anymore? And that wasn't the worst. In his blood, he pictured the virus marching toward his lungs, filling them with cauliflower-like lumps of grey and green mold until he couldn't inhale.
>
> Did that breath hurt? He wheezed a little as the air whispered from his mouth. Was that breath just a little bit harder than the last? He didn't know. He didn't know.

Rearranging Style

Rewrite either Lubar's or Van Pelt's excerpt and do all you can to erase or change the voice by changing the style.

Then try the same thing with a scene from a book you like.

Distinctive style. Now you've read three authors, three styles. Vega, Lubar, Van Pelt. Each style is distinct—so distinct that if you saw another example of writing from them you might be able to match the example to the writer without being told which author wrote what excerpt.

But what if they squashed their own style and tried to write like someone else? What if Vega tried to write like Van Pelt or Van Pelt tried to write like Vega? What if Lubar stopped using ironic humor? The things that make each writer special would be lost.

Your style. In the end, it's not writing like other people that will make your story stand out. It's writing like yourself. It's pouring your own heart and mind into what you say and how you say it.

Experimenting With Style

Write two paragraphs of a scene between a couple of characters. Then play with the style, rewriting the paragraphs. Don't worry about whether you're writing well or not. This is just for you. Try writing in a humorous style. Then an emotional style. Then poetic. Then matter-of-fact.

Is there a style that fits you really well? If so, write some more in that style to deepen your connection with it.

Differences. We've all had times of feeling separated from others somehow, of feeling different or unusual in ways that stand out or made us uncomfortable. That feeling can be like a rusty nail digging into your foot—especially if you feel lonely or outcast. It can hurt in a way that seems it won't ever heal. Sharp, deep, and worse with every step.

But when it comes to writing great stories, the rusty nail can transform into a magic shoe. You can take what's different about you and then build upon it to create unusual characters, the sort who are fascinating to read about. Dramatic.

Characters Set Apart

Pick a favorite book or movie. When you think about the characters, what do you find that's unusual or different about each one? How do those differences help define the characters? Now imagine the characters without those differences. What would happen to the story?

Building Your Story

Bring your protagonist and antagonist to mind. Have you allowed them to be different/unusual? What stands out about them?

Write a scene in which your protagonist or antagonist is forced to show a difference that makes him or her feel uncomfortable.

Writer's block. Sometimes writing is easy, and the words pour out in a flow that feels as if it will be endless and effortless. But sometimes when writers least expect it, they suddenly stumble over a big concrete block that seems to have fallen across their path out of nowhere. Ouch!

I used to have a misconception that teen writers never feel blocked. But now I've heard from enough teens asking, "How do you deal with writer's block?" to know that teens aren't immune.

What is this insidious writer's affliction? Why is writer's block so common that there's a name for it and everyone's heard of it? Why not zoologist's block, welder's block, doctor's block?

All I can say is, it's not the easiest thing in the world to dig into your own heart, mind, and guts for a story and then come up with a way to write it down.

Signs of writer's block. How do you know if you have writer's block? Here are some symptoms and signs:

- **You can't write.** People assume writer's block always means "can't write." However, it's not usually a complete blackout. Every once in a while, yes, true night falls. When that happens, nothing is there. Nothing. This is frightening, disturbing, and painful.

- **You don't like what you've written.** You think everything you write is trash someone should have left at the curb. This is a more popular form of writer's block. (It's totally normal to feel this way. Either that or I'm completely abnormal and so are my writer friends.)

- **You are anxious about moving forward.** This frequently happens in the middle of a story. Despair sets in. You think, "The story's going nowhere, and I don't know what happens next." So instead of writing the next scene, you go back and rewrite old scenes again and again. Or you sit mournfully in a cocoon of misery, believing creativity has forsaken you.

- **You think you'll never be able to write again.** Even if you just finished a story, you believe you'll never be able to write another. (I thought I was alone in this feeling until I started listening to other writers. One of them had written forty-nine books and still felt that she wouldn't be able to write fifty.)

Getting past writer's block. So what do writers do about writer's block? Most of us have a variety of strategies, and there isn't any one solution. Here are a few possibilities you might try:

- **Take a break.** If there's nothing there, maybe it's time to give it a rest. Overloaded is overloaded. Your condition is temporary.

- **Address it.** Talk back to the block as if it's an annoying pest—which it is. ("Go away and let me write." "Get out of here!" "Who asked you?")

- **Don't panic.** If you're dreading writing the next scene because you don't know what happens next, remember that there *is* a solution, and your imagination is capable of finding it. Just because you don't know now doesn't mean you won't know *ever*. Step away from the story if necessary. Ask your unconscious mind to work on the problem for awhile.

    One thing that can help to enlist the unconscious mind is to put a notebook next to your bed. Before going to sleep, write a question you want your unconscious mind to work with. It could be very general: "How do I get over my writer's block?" Or it could be specific to a story: "Why does Evie fear Jerome?"

    Actually write the question down rather than simply thinking it. This signals your unconscious mind that it's important to you. When you wake up, jot down your impressions. As you go through your day, you may find solutions popping into your mind.

    Don't worry if this doesn't work the first time you try it. Like most things, it may take a bit of practice.

- **Remember who you really are.** You are an imaginative person. Even if your imagination seems to have disappeared, it's still there, just hiding. Why would it go into hiding? Often, it's running from the twin demons of doubt and fear.

  Creative work by its nature puts us into the realm of uncertainty. It is about reaching into the unknown and touching the mystery. We can't predict the outcome in advance.

  Few creative writers are immune to feelings of fear when setting out into the unknown. Even if we've taken a journey before and come back with a great story, the new journey involves a new unknown. If it didn't, storytelling would become formulaic; it wouldn't require touching the mystery anymore.

  I believe that when writers feel blocked, doubt and fear about the unknown have become stronger than trust in imagination. This is perfectly normal, but dwelling on doubts and fears only reinforces them.

  It can really help to dwell on something other than our fears—to remind ourselves again and again that imagination is truly unlimited, and it has the power to open new doorways.

  When a block seems to enclose you and you feel like you can't write, it may help to relax as much as you can and trust your creative imagination to come up with something you haven't considered yet.

  And please be patient with yourself.

- **Feed your artistic self.** Take a walk, visit a friend, watch a movie, listen to music, get a little sunshine. What nourishes the artist within you?

- **Focus on colors, sounds, tastes, smells, textures.** Some writers stare at the sky or play music that reminds them of the story they want to write. I sometimes chew on a cinnamon stick or take a big whiff of peppermint to jolt my senses. You might decide to talk wordlessly with your hands, or squeeze your little brother's playdough.

- **Add some props.** Anything a writer can do to bring the storyland closer can help. If you're writing about locker rooms, don't be afraid to keep smelly socks handy. If your character is a doctor, look for an old stethoscope at a garage sale. Because I write fantasy, I have a crystal ball and a

It's not the easiest thing in the world to dig into your own heart, mind, and guts for a story and then come up with a way to write it down.

sword at home. Pictures on my walls remind me of the lands I visit while writing.

- **Write at unusual times or in unusual places.** I find that getting up at 4 a.m. is usually enough to pulverize any block. Maybe it's because my critical mind hasn't had a chance to wake up yet and I can run to the story and get there first.

  Also, it's helpful to change settings—like writing in a coffee shop or in the basement or next to a tree.

- **Try more freewriting.** Maybe you aren't giving yourself a zone that's free of criticism. Now, more than ever, you need that zone. If you notice that you're being your own harshest critic, ease up. (And don't criticize yourself for being critical!)

  Let your writing flow, flow, flow. Write out the doubt and fear. Write through to the other side.

It takes guts to put your heart into your writing and keep going when you feel blocked. But it's worth it. And by moving ahead, putting your own personality into your writing—including what sets you apart—you show what you have to give that no one else has got.

Your voice.

Feed your artistic self.

WRITING DIALOGUE

CHAPTER SIX

WRITING DIALOGUE

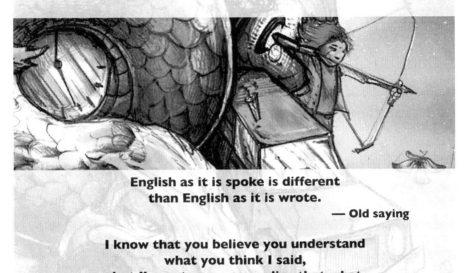

English as it is spoke is different than English as it is wrote.
— Old saying

I know that you believe you understand what you think I said, but I'm not sure you realize that what you heard is not what I meant.
— Robert McCloskey

Dialogue can do so much for a story. It reveals character and relationships, enhances tension, and moves the plot.

In daily life, we chatter and babble, fumble for words, say "uh," wander from one sentence to the next taking tangents, and sometimes never get to the point. "Hogan said he wants to show me…uh, y'know, sometimes I wonder if he ever means a word he says. There was this one time that he told me he was going to meet me at…where was it? The fountain? No, not the fountain…oh no, not again…where did I put my phone? Have you seen it?"

But in fiction, every word of dialogue counts. And a few techniques can make the difference between a story that's just okay and a story that really springs to life.

Dialogue versus narrative. In dialogue, characters talk. ("Nothing ever happens in this town," he said.)

With narrative, the author tells the reader what's going on. (It was a quiet little town. Some might call it boring.)

In the examples below, the same information is given in two different ways, first as dialogue and then as narrative. Which is more interesting to read?

Dialogue:

"Why won't you let me help you?" Sophia felt like pounding her fists on Jeff's chest. Why was he so stubborn?

Jeff shrugged. "I never had nobody before. Don't need no one now."

Narrative:

Jeff grew up lonely, without anyone to rely on. His parents took little interest in him, and he had no real friends. When Sophia tried to help him, he wouldn't accept it. This frustrated her.

Dialogue:

"I've got Beeler for English," Cassie said. "What's he like?"

"Horrible!" Lou cried. "So boring you'll have to stick toothpicks in your eyes to stay awake. Nothing like Huggins."

Cassie gathered her books. "I don't care if I have to spend the day in the office. I'm getting a transfer."

Narrative:

Cassie found out Mr. Beeler would be her English teacher for the year. When Lou said Beeler was boring, Cassie decided to try for a transfer.

USING DIALOGUE TO REVEAL CHARACTERS AND RELATIONSHIPS

Characters show their personalities by the way they express themselves in dialogue. Here are some examples:

"Look, here comes Daniel," Corrie said, nudging Jennifer. "Do you think he'll notice you?"

"I'll die right now, right here in the middle of this hallway if he doesn't," Jennifer answered.

"Matt!" the coach called, running up red-faced, "Why aren't you ready? The race starts in two minutes."

In fiction, every word of dialogue counts.

"Sorry," Matt mumbled. "I can't run."

"Why?" The coach was practically screaming in his face.

"I can't find my lucky coin. I'll lose."

Tad looked glumly at the graphs. "This is one hundred percent wrong," he said.

"It just needs a little tweaking," Michael answered.

"We'll have to redo the entire thing and recalculate."

Michael shrugged. "Or we could adjust one variable and call it good."

The dialogue shows that Jennifer is a bit of a drama queen, and Matt is extremely superstitious. Tad is a pessimistic perfectionist, while Michael lacks integrity.

Dialogue can also be used to reveal information about relationships between characters. The following examples show people in various relationships:

"Why don't you wear that cute little pink outfit that goes so well with your coloring?" Tami's mother asked.

"This? You've got to be kidding. Pink!" Tami yanked the hanger off the rack and threw it on the floor. "Stay out of my closet, Mom."

Rudy's dad scowled when he saw the new video game. "How much did that stupid thing cost?"

"What do you care?" Rudy grumbled. "I earned it."

"Good for you. Now you can start paying your own car insurance."

"I'd like to go out with you, but I have to mow the lawn and clean my room," Jordan told Amber.

"Since when do you mow the lawn or clean your room—ever?" Amber's voice squeaked in his ear.

"Since now." Jordan glared straight ahead.

"I'd do anything for you," Ellie told Dominic, pushing the words past the boulder in her throat.

"Do you know where Marie is?" Dominic asked, staring past Ellie's shoulder.

"Anything." Ellie's voice rasped and then faded to a whisper. "I mean it."

The dialogue tells us Tami resents her mother treating her like a child. Rudy and his father don't see eye to eye about money. Jordan is angry with Amber and trying to avoid her, and Dominic is not at all interested in the desperate Ellie.

Remember Todd Mitchell's scene about Cinderella's stepsister on page 26? Here's just the dialogue section from that scene:

When Mom asked me to cut off my toes, I wasn't very surprised.

"I only want what's best for you," she said, dragging a hair across the edge of the butcher's knife. The blade, newly sharpened, split the hair in half. "Life is full of suffering," she said. "I pluck my eyebrows every morning. This will only hurt for a moment, and then we'll be set for life."

She handed the butcher's knife to me and indicated the chopping block that she'd placed an old curtain under to keep the blood from staining the floor.

"Go on then," she said, glancing nervously at the door to the living room where the prince was waiting. "And don't scream. If he hears you, he might suspect something."

In Mitchell's dialogue, the stepsister never says a word. Do you wish she would speak up, yell, scream, protest? What is she saying with her silence?

Showing Personality Through Dialogue

Imagine a crowded fast food restaurant. Pick several imaginary characters with very different personalities. Put words in their mouths as they order food or talk to their friends.

Then ask a friend to decide what kind of personalities the characters have, based on what you've written.

Dialogue can reveal relationships.

BRACKETS AND TAGS

Dialogue brackets. Descriptions that surround dialogue, such as "Tami yanked the hanger off the rack and threw it on the floor" or "Ellie's voice rasped and then faded to a whisper," are known as "brackets." Brackets give information about the emotion behind the words being spoken, so the way you bracket your dialogue has a big impact on meaning.

The following examples show how the same piece of dialogue has different meanings, depending on the brackets:

- When they reached the summit, he stood on the rim of the world. "I love you," he shouted, and his words seemed to echo from mountain to mountain.

- She slid a full teacup across the polished table in front of him. "I love you," she said breathlessly.

- Anita downed the rest of her orange juice in one gulp. "I love you," she yelled over her shoulder as she raced out the door.

- "I love you," Aunt Velma said vaguely, squinting down at her menu.

- When he flicked on the flashlight, the beam played across giant stalagmites. "I love you," he mumbled in Laura's direction, and then peered into a recess of the cave.

- He pulled the tattered gray blanket over her shoulders. "I love you," he said.

Dialogue tags. Dialogue tags are phrases like *he said* or *she said*. There are dozens of tags available, such as *replied, responded, shouted, answered, asked, yelled, cried, called, whispered, sobbed, snarled, laughed…* (Some writers say words cannot be snarled or laughed and insist the correct format is *he said, snarling* or *she said, laughing*—but most readers are fine with *he snarled* or *she laughed*.)

Descriptions that surround dialogue are known as "brackets."

There are hundreds of adverbs, too, which can become part of a dialogue tag: she said *angrily, haughtily, repressively, snippily, timidly, hesitantly, darkly…*

So which tags are most effective?

It depends.

Generally, simple is best—*he said* and *she said*—with *he asked* and *she answered* used occasionally. *Said, asked,* and *answered* tend to disappear in the reader's mind, highlighting the dialogue itself.

Too many fancy tags can become distracting and even annoying:

> "What are you doing here?" she inquired.
> "Looking for you," he replied.
> "Why?" she questioned.
> "Because Ted's back in town," he responded.

No tag at all makes the dialogue stand out, and readers can follow several lines of dialogue before they need to be reminded of who is talking:

> "What are you doing here?" she asked.
> "Looking for you."
> "Why?"
> "Because Ted's back in town."

Adverbs can quickly become excessive:

> "What are you doing here?" she asked timidly.
> "Looking for you," he said purposefully.
> "Why?" she ventured unhappily.
> "Because Ted's back in town," he said pointedly.

If the meaning is clear from the dialogue itself, then adding tags with verbs and adverbs is redundant:

> "You fool!" she shouted angrily.

The exclamation point already tells us she's shouting, and the fact that she's shouting an insult tells us she's angry. A bracket would be more effective:

"You fool!" Violet ran out the door, slamming it behind her.

But if you wanted to deliver a different feeling than what the words actually say, a verb/adverb tag would be helpful:

"You fool," Violet whispered mischievously.

SUBTEXT

If your car breaks down late at night and you wake your best friend with a call to come get you, he might show up scowling. He might say your car has never been worth the gas it guzzles. On the surface, he's angry. But there's more to it.

There is subtext. Subtext is information that is implied, not stated outright. In the example above, what is the subtext? A real friend has gone out of his way for you.

Dialogue and brackets can be a great way to show subtext:

"You promised you'd go with us tonight," Elliott said. He folded his arms. (Subtext: *I plan to hold you to your promise.*)

"I never said that." Johnny tried to look Elliott in the face but somehow his eyes kept slipping and he ended up staring at his shoes. (Subtext: *I'm not a good liar. I wish I had never promised to go. I'm afraid of you.*)

Elliott took a step closer. "Maybe someone else promised?" (Subtext: *Liar. Don't even think about backing out.*)

Johnny swallowed. "There's a red moon," he said, pointing to the sky. (Subtext: *I'm superstitious and scared half to death. I don't want to go anywhere tonight.*)

Writing Subtext

Write a conversation that reveals the subtext in a situation full of undercurrents between two people. Here is one situation you might try:

Two good friends are competing for the same prize. Each desperately wants to win. Each also believes that the other is more qualified.

Dialogue tags are phrases like "he said" and "she said."

COMMON PROBLEMS
WITH DIALOGUE

By avoiding the common dialogue problems described below, you will keep the conversations between your characters going strong.

Dialogue is contrived and sounds artificial. Here's an example:

> "I'm going to ask your father about it when he gets back from his business trip. He travels a lot, you know, and he's coming back tonight," Becky's mother told her.
> "He does travel a lot," Becky said. "And it's always on business."

The writer wants the reader to know that Becky's father travels a lot and is about to return from a trip. But would a daughter need to be told why and how often her father travels?

Here's the same dialogue, worded more authentically:

> "I'll ask your father when he gets back tonight," Becky's mother told her.
> "I wish he wasn't gone so much," Becky answered. "He loves his job more than me."

Another example of contrived dialogue:

> "Since we arrived in New York City six weeks ago I've been looking for a job, and I haven't found one," Lori told her mother.
> "I hope you find one tomorrow," said her mother. "Let's get started on watering the vegetables that we planted yesterday in the window box, in hopes we can grow some lettuce and carrots."

Characters wouldn't talk that way—it's stilted and unreal.

More believable:

"Six weeks I've been looking!" Lori shut the empty cupboard with a bang. "No one will hire me. I'm not sophisticated enough for New York City."

Her mother shook her head. "I'm going to water the vegetables." She stalked out of the kitchen. Lori stared after her. What a silly idea, planting veggies in a window box.

This example of dialogue from author Teresa R. Funke sounds natural but still provides information:

They continued exploring the camp, stopping just short of the electric fence to gaze beyond the lock-jawed guards toward the hazy skies above Shanghai, less than fifteen miles away. "Maybe we can escape," Marty said.

"If we could get to the city, we could find us a boat," Patrick said.

"The Japanese control the harbor," Colin reminded him.

"Okay, we could bribe some Chinese peasant to hide us on his boat."

"With what money?"

"We could steal some."

Arthur shook his head. "Fact is, fellas, we wouldn't make it to the city. We'd stick out like sore thumbs among all those Chinese. Besides, what about our groups of ten? You heard what the guards said when they numbered us off. If one of our group escapes, the other nine will be shot."

"They wouldn't dare," Patrick said.

"Want to bet?"

—excerpt from *Remember Wake*, by Teresa R. Funke

Dialogue doesn't ring true for the characters. Here is an example:

Marla loved spending the long summer days in her vegetable garden.

"I'm glad we had a chance to get the cucumber seeds in the ground today," she said, brushing dirt from her hands and smiling at her daughter. "Won't it be fun to see the shoots come up tomorrow?"

"I can't wait," Dorene agreed.

Characters shouldn't talk in a way that is stilted and unreal.

An experienced gardener would plant seeds in the spring, not the summer, and she would know that cucumbers take five or six days to germinate, not one day.

Another example:

"I think mom is really stressed from the divorce and that's why she's been feeding us so many Tater Tots," three-year-old Gilly said.

"Tater Tots are better than nothing," her sister told her. "Do we have any milk?"

"I think there's some at the back of the fridge, but it may have spoiled. I'll check the date."

A three-year-old doesn't analyze motives or wonder if milk has gone bad. The same conversation would make sense if Gilly were twelve instead of three.

Dialogue is long-winded, boring the reader. Putting in too much dialogue, however realistic, slows the action of the story to the speed of a slug on a glacier. Here is an example:

"Hello?"

"Hey, Brad. How's it going?"

"All right. What's up with you?"

"Nothing much. But I wanted to ask you about something."

"What?"

"Can you meet me at the cemetery on Sunday?"

In a story, the only line you would need is the last one. The rest wouldn't serve the story.

When writing, I find it helpful to write out all the dialogue I'm thinking and then go back and trim it. Here's an example of dialogue before trimming:

"I'm wondering if I should try calling Derek tomorrow." Meredith fiddled with her fork, pushing a piece of limp red lettuce around her plate. "I've been thinking about calling him for three weeks but then something keeps happening to stop me. I've had way too much on my mind."

"You still haven't called him?" Justin stared at his half-eaten sandwich. "You said you were for sure going to call him last weekend."

"Yeah, but when I call I want to be feeling good about myself. I felt bad about myself last weekend, so I didn't call."

"You keep saying you're going to call."

"I know. Sometimes I really believe I'm losing my mind."

The same dialogue after trimming:

"I should call Derek." Meredith fiddled with her fork, pushing a piece of limp red lettuce around her plate.

"You still haven't called him?" Justin stared at his half-eaten sandwich.

"Sometimes I really believe I'm losing my mind."

Cutting Dialogue Down to Size

Write an exchange of dialogue between two characters, putting down every thought you have. Then trim it, keeping only what is necessary.

Dialogue shows characters talking alike. You don't speak like your best friend, your boss, your hair stylist, or your teacher. The people in your life have unique speech patterns and gestures. Characters in stories need voices and gestures of their own, too.

Here is an example of dialogue where the speech patterns and gestures aren't distinct enough to separate the characters:

"I really hope you get there in time," Curt said, opening the car door for Ed.

"I really hope I do too," Ed answered. He stooped to put his duffel bag in the backseat. "But I have a long way to go."

"Do you think she'll wait for you?"

"Maybe she will, but I don't know." Ed got behind the wheel.

Dialogue that is long-winded can bore the reader.

Here's the scene with more emphasis on individual mannerisms and styles of speech:

"I hope you get there in time," Curt said, brushing his hair back from his face with a sweaty hand.

Ed frowned. "Me too." He jerked open the car door and threw his duffle in the backseat.

"Do you think she'll wait for you?"

"Don't know." Ed slithered behind the wheel and turned the key.

Bringing Out Character With Gestures and Speech

Write a conversation between two characters. Emphasize differences in their gestures and speech patterns so that the characters are clearly distinct.

DIALOGUE FORMAT

Although a few famous writers do not use standard dialogue format, most do. Here's what's standard for dialogue:

Put periods, commas, question marks, and exclamation points inside double quotation marks. Create a new paragraph each time separate characters speak, like this:

He said, "I'm so excited to be writing a book."

"I'm beyond excited." She laughed in his face.

"I've been writing every day," he said, "and I plan to finish my book before you finish yours."

"I'm almost done!" she cried.

"How's that possible?" He raised an eyebrow.

Characters in stories need voices and gestures of their own. When characters speak up, they enliven a story.

Note that dialogue tags after an exclamation or question mark are not capitalized. ("I'm almost done!" she cried.) But bracket sentences *do* begin with a capital. ("How's that possible?" He raised an eyebrow.)

When paraphrasing what someone said, don't use quotation marks at all:

> He said that he was excited to be writing a book.

Inner dialogue. Inner dialogue is when a character's thoughts are written out for the reader. Thoughts may or may not be enclosed in quotation marks. Often, however, italics are used to set off inner dialogue:

> The moon looked cold and far off, as if it were trying to distance itself. Even the trees drew back, and the mountains receded. *I'll never get there,* she thought.

Building Your Story

Write a page of dialogue between your protagonist and antagonist. Use brackets, tags, and subtext to give a strong sense of who the characters are.

In life, have you ever kept silent or fumbled for words and then played the situation over in your mind and thought of exactly the right thing to say—but the moment was long gone? This doesn't have to happen to your characters. One of the best things about writing dialogue is putting words in characters' mouths—the perfect words for the situation they're in.

When characters speak up, they enliven a story. And writing those conversations can enliven the writer, too.

Put periods, commas, question marks, and exclamation points inside double quotation marks.

SHOWING AND TELLING

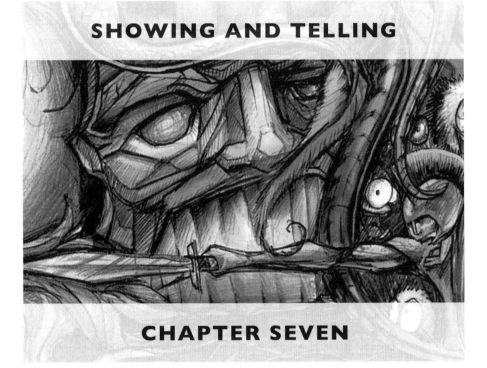

CHAPTER SEVEN

SHOWING AND TELLING

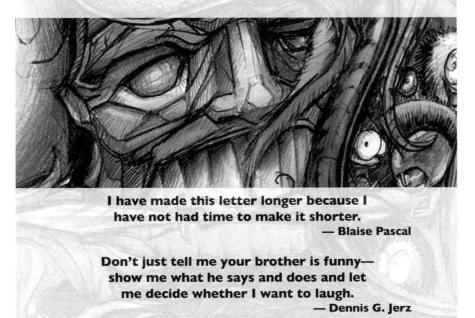

I have made this letter longer because I have not had time to make it shorter.
— **Blaise Pascal**

Don't just tell me your brother is funny—show me what he says and does and let me decide whether I want to laugh.
— **Dennis G. Jerz**

If you've taken writing classes, you've heard the advice to "show, don't tell." The heart of this idea is well expressed by Mark Twain, who said, "Don't say the old lady screamed—bring her on and let her scream."

When *showing*, writers describe characters doing and saying things. They let readers figure out for themselves what it all means.

When *telling*, writers give information to the reader in narrative form. In other words, they just tell readers what's going on.

The following scene is written in *showing* mode. Notice how the characters are doing and saying things:

Showing

Janey drew the curtain aside and peered out the rain-drenched window at Darvis as he splashed through the puddles. He wore thick boots but he was bareheaded.

Janey tapped on the window glass and then turned to her uncle. "I'm telling you," she said. "Darvis is a rainmaker."

Uncle John blew out a long breath and settled more deeply into his recliner. "I've had a long day. Don't make it longer."

"The rain started the day Darvis got here," Janey said. "It hasn't stopped since. You're always telling me water's white gold. We could

make him welcome in Covington and then you could persuade the City
Council to build a bigger reservoir."

Uncle John folded his arms. "Girl, you oughta write a novel."

Here's the same scene, this time in *telling* mode. Notice how the actions and
conversations are left out. Instead, everything is narrated.

Ever since Darvis came to Covington, Janey had watched him closely. The more she saw of him the more sure she became that he was the
reason the rain kept falling. The rain clouds had arrived the day he moved
to town and never lifted.

Janey tried hard to tell her Uncle John about Darvis. Her uncle served
on the City Planning Commission, and Janey thought he might be able
to persuade the city to build a bigger reservoir in Covington. Uncle John
always said that water was white gold. Janey thought they should make
Darvis welcome, and then Covington would have plenty of water.

But the more Janey talked about Darvis, the more Uncle John rolled
his eyes. Janey couldn't get through to him.

The first *showing* scene seems more alive because showing makes things feel
like they're happening here and now. When narration goes on for too long, the
story can lag. The action feels as if it's happening somewhere else at some other
time.

Here are a couple more examples that illustrate the difference between showing and telling:

Showing:

Fahd threw himself into motion. Giving a sharp whistle, he pushed
Maeve to the ground and stood in front of her. Jasper motioned urgently
to Evan to duck beside the boulder. The boy crouched just as an arrow
flashed through the air where he'd been standing.

Jasper leaped toward Maeve. Fahd caught him and flung him aside.
"Stay down," the soldier ordered. "You're not fit to fight."

Telling:

> Fahd took charge, guarding Maeve and whistling for the rest of the guard. Evan was nearly killed by an arrow that landed in the spot where he'd been standing seconds earlier. Jasper wanted to join the fight, but Fahd wouldn't let him, ordering him to keep out of it because he wasn't fit.

Showing:

> Screams from the bleachers blared across the gym like a bad sound track. Jarrod shook the stinging sweat from his eyes, his hand a blur as he slapped the ball faster and faster, pounding down the court.

Telling:

> The crowd in the gym got caught up watching the basketball game. Jarrod played so hard he was sweating.

A place for showing. As we saw in the dialogue chapter, conversations themselves are more captivating than summaries of conversations—and dialogue is one aspect of showing. Action scenes can show what's going on. When you take readers straight into the action, they feel like they're part of what's happening. This is far more exciting than just being told about it.

Another important part of showing is allowing readers to figure out what a character is like. So instead of *telling* the reader that *Bonnie was courageous,* you would write a scene *showing* Bonnie's actions as she stands up for her friends. Instead of *Dean made everybody laugh,* you would put funny words in Dean's mouth. Instead of *Erica was timid and shy,* you would describe a tongue-tied Erica blushing and looking down at the floor.

A place for telling. In fiction, it's important to hit the highlights. What do I mean by highlights? Well, suppose you had only five minutes to tell your life story. You would automatically hit the highlights. You would summarize or skip many things.

Narration can keep a story on track by summarizing the parts that aren't highlights. Sometimes a writer needs to say things such as, "Half a year went by

When narration goes on for a long time, the story can start to lag.

and the only change he noticed was the seasons." At those times, *telling* is an important tool.

It can also be used to give readers colorful information about characters:

Allie needed sunshine every day. Without it, she grew thorns.

Brent would rather get ten tattoos and a tongue piercing than eat a formal dinner with his aunt and uncle.

Karin could turn five kinds of leftovers into a gourmet meal.

Although this kind of writing is technically telling, it adds sparkle and zest when it's sprinkled in with showing.

Building Your Story

Using only telling mode, write an action scene involving your protagonist and antagonist.

Then rewrite the scene using only showing. One way to do this is by thinking of the scene like a play. Describe the setting through the senses. Describe what people say and do.

PLOTTING AND SCHEMING

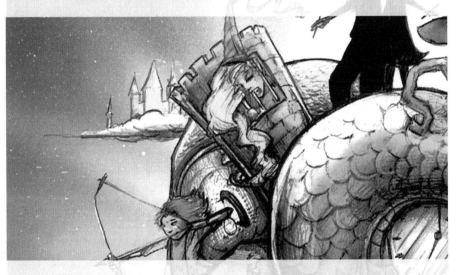

CHAPTER EIGHT

PLOTTING AND SCHEMING

**Writing a novel is like driving a car at night.
You can see only as far as your headlights,
but you can make the whole trip that way.**
— E. L. Doctorow

Nothing will work unless you do.
— Maya Angelou

The first time someone asked, "How did you come up with the plot for *The Seer and the Sword?*" I answered with true eloquence.

"Uh," I said. "Umm…uh."

When I'm writing fiction I don't know the direction my plots will take. For me, plotting is like the rest of writing—it doesn't make sense until the story is finished. After I've arrived at the end, the plot becomes visible.

I've concluded that plotting takes both creative intuition and logic. Intuition is the part of us that can know things without knowing how we know them. Logic reasons things out.

Creative intuition is important because it can connect things that didn't start out to be connected, things that logic would never bring together—such as cyclones and emerald cities (*The Wonderful Wizard of Oz*) or wooden puppets and real boys (*Pinocchio*). How reasonable is it for a boy to lose his shadow (*Peter Pan*)? How reasonable is it that a shoe would fit only one young woman in a whole kingdom ("Cinderella")? And yet, these unreasonable connections form the basis for enduring stories.

Logic, too, is important to the process of plotting. Logic can pull together the elements of fiction you've been studying and use them to support a plot. Logic can analyze a story and point out the pieces that need to be cut, the pieces that need to be kept, and the pieces that need to be added.

On the side of logic, there's an excellent book that analyzes plot structure. It's called *The Seven Basic Plots* (London: Continuum, 2004), by Christopher Booker, and it's a book I highly recommend. According to Booker, there are seven basic plots that are repeated over and over in various stories throughout the ages. (Booker 3–8) He goes into much more depth with each one, but here I've paraphrased the basics:

Overcoming the Monster. In this plot, the hero learns of a dreadful monster of some sort that is terrorizing the land. This monster can be human (a serial killer for instance), or it can be an actual monster like Dracula. After hearing about the monster, the hero decides there must be a way it can be overcome. Then severe setbacks occur as the monster proves it's even worse than reports have indicated. Eventually there's an extreme ordeal for the hero, who then has a "thrilling escape" from death. In the end, the hero kills or otherwise defeats the monster. Examples: *Dracula* (Bram Stoker) and *The Three Musketeers* (Alexandre Dumas). (Booker 27–28, 37, 48–49)

Rags to Riches. In this plot, the hero starts out poor or obscure in some way—wretched, mistreated, and scorned. Then comes a glimpse of success and the possibility of glories to come. Right after that, everything goes wrong. The hero is absolutely miserable and separated from what he or she hopes to find. Self-discovery follows. The hero develops inner strength and confronts what is holding him or her back. In the end, fulfillment arrives. The hero ends up rich and famous or at least deeply appreciated, all as a result of inner qualities that have been developed or revealed. Examples: "The Ugly Duckling" (Hans Christian Andersen) and "Cinderella" (Brothers Grimm). (Booker 56, 58, 65–66)

The Quest. In this plot, the hero learns of a treasure or a promised land that's far away and decides to make a journey. Companions are chosen to go along. The journey turns out to be fraught with mounting dangers. Along with danger and disaster, the hero and his or her companions find valuable help and advice about how to keep going. Near the end of the quest, the hero must face an ordeal so intense and difficult that attaining the treasure or promised land seems truly impossible. Tested to the fullest, the hero survives, proving himself or herself worthy of the prize.

There are seven basic plots that get repeated over and over.

In the end, the goal is won. The treasure is found or the new kingdom is established. Examples: *The Lord of the Rings* (J. R. R. Tolkien), *The Odyssey* (Homer), and *Watership Down* (Richard Adams). (Booker 69–72, 83)

Voyage and Return. In this plot, the hero is thrown into an unknown world after experiencing an earth-shattering event that takes him or her out of familiar territory. The hero explores the new world but never feels at home there, despite discovering amazing wonders. Then an evil force or "shadow" makes its presence known, bringing about frustration and hardships. The shadow almost takes over, and then the hero makes a death-defying escape and returns home wiser. Examples: *The Wonderful Wizard of Oz* (L. Frank Baum), *Peter Pan* (J. M. Barrie) and *Alice's Adventures in Wonderland* (Lewis Carroll). (Booker 88–89, 105–106)

Comedy. To understand the fifth type of plot, we have to set aside the sense we already have of what a comedy is. Most of us think of a comedy as something that makes us laugh. But in Booker's analysis (and in classic plays such as those of Shakespeare), a comedy is simply a story with a happy ending, a story that follows a particular structure. Though it usually has funny moments, they aren't the focus of the story, which goes something like this: One or more characters are trapped in a life situation that seems bleak and frustrating. The "true nature" of one or more of these characters is hidden, and people suited for each other are separated by misunderstandings. Then characters experience a change of heart, true natures are revealed, and things are sorted out. Misunderstandings clear up, bringing happiness and union of lovers and friends. Examples: *Pride and Prejudice* (Jane Austen) and *Much Ado About Nothing* (Shakespeare). (Booker 117–118, 133, 150)

Tragedy. In tragedies, protagonists cast about cluelessly for a while and then focus on something they want. They commit to action, but things go wrong. Then things get very bad. Then worse. Despair sets in, and the protagonist is destroyed, by death or other forces. Examples: *Julius Caesar* and *Romeo and Juliet* (Shakespeare). (Booker 156–157, 166, 189)

Rebirth. With this plot, the hero falls under an oppressive force of some sort, but for a while this threat may appear to be contained or neutralized. Then the threat grows and gets much, much worse until the hero is enduring a living hell. The oppressive force seems triumphant. Then the hero at last sees the light, is redeemed and brought into a more heavenly existence. Examples: "The Frog Prince" and "Sleeping Beauty" (Brothers Grimm), and *A Christmas Carol* (Charles Dickens). (Booker 193, 195, 198, 204)

Endless variety. Seven plots don't sound like many until you realize there can be endless variety within each of the seven. How many monsters might be conjured by a vivid imagination? In how many ways might a character be miserable and undone? What daunting quests and voyages might call for assorted heroes to go on mighty adventures? Infinite numbers.

Human beings are always eager for new twists to ancient plot lines. As you travel the storytelling path, you'll find fresh angles, add ingenious switchbacks, and create compelling crossroads of your own.

Cause and effect. No matter which of the seven plots your story follows, cause and effect will be important.

The boy hid in the kitchen cupboard next to the flour barrels. That sentence, though halfway interesting, contains no plot line because it doesn't demonstrate cause and effect.

When the kitchen fell under attack, the boy hid in the cupboard next to the flour barrels. Now we have cause and effect, and the beginnings of a plot line.

In a story, one action leads to another, which leads to another. *Because the boy hid in the cupboard, he survived the attack. Because he witnessed the attack, he could recognize the killers.*

And so on.

Naturally, different characters won't respond to the same situation in the same way. They'll take action according to who they are. A reckless boy won't hide. A foolish boy won't be frightened. A more terrified boy won't be able to move.

Whatever your characters do in one scene leads them to the next. Scenes keep building on each other, gathering momentum.

There's more to come about plotting. The next chapter deals with conflict and complications, both important to any plot because they get you through the middle of the story and lead you on to the end.

Looking at Plots

Think about your favorite novels. Which plot lines do you think they follow?

Choose one novel. Can you trace one of Booker's plot lines through the novel from beginning to end?

Another idea: Pick one of the basic plots and use it as the basis for a story of your own.

Building Your Story

If you've finished writing a story, try checking it against Booker's plot lines. Or if you're partway through writing a story, what direction does the plot seem to be taking?

In a story, one action leads to another, which leads to another.

CONFLICTS, MIDDLES, AND ENDS

CHAPTER NINE

CONFLICTS, MIDDLES, AND ENDS

Heap hazards on their heads.
— Kurt Vonnegut

**You know you've read a good book when you turn
the last page and feel as if you've lost a friend.**
— Zora Neale Hurston

Conflict is one of the most important ingredients in fiction. Without it, stories are like cars without engines. They just sit there.

No one wants to read about a wonderful guy who meets a darling girl, and they have a perfectly lovely day and then a great year.

Good stories are filled with conflict that begins early and ends late. Conflict revs up the action and keeps readers interested in what might happen next. In fiction, ease and happiness kill the story. Characters must go through hardships and pain.

Making your characters miserable is harder than it sounds. We grow to love our characters and don't want them to suffer. But suffer they must.

When J. K. Rowling wrote about Harry Potter in *Harry Potter and the Sorcerer's Stone*, she didn't describe a wizard nurtured in a loving family and given everything he might need to understand himself and his heritage. Harry lives under the stairs in a closet and has no idea who he really is.

When Stephenie Meyer wrote about Isabella Swan in *Twilight*, she didn't just tell a story about a young woman in love. Isabella falls for someone so dangerous he himself warns her he might kill her. Even so, she feels completely unable to stop herself from becoming more and more entangled.

When Suzanne Collins wrote *The Hunger Games*, she didn't only create hardship and oppression for Katniss Everdeen. Katniss risks her life to save her little sister, but that's just the beginning. By the end of the series, Katniss has endured so many horrifying experiences that her sanity is also on the line.

These conflicts in the lives of the characters serve to propel their stories forward and deepen the reader's involvement.

The power of conflict. I could describe something completely ordinary, like a chocolate ice cream cone. Even if I described the cone beautifully and went into detail about its creaminess, most readers wouldn't care about it. But if a bystander jostled the cone and the ice cream landed splat on the floor, things would get slightly more interesting. And then, if the person who caused the splat began to snicker and sneer…suddenly there might be a scene worth reading.

That's the power of conflict. Like a charismatic actor, there's something about conflict that gets our attention every time it appears.

Think about your favorite books and movies. What conflicts are present for the characters? And what would the story be like if the conflict weren't there?

External and internal conflict. There are two main types of conflict—external and internal. External conflict forces characters into trials and dangers coming from outside themselves. Internal conflict is conflict that arises inside a character.

Here are some kinds of external conflict:

- **Conflict with antagonists** *(person vs. person).* Antagonistic characters can be human, animal, or fantasy creatures. They try to keep protagonists from achieving their goals. Sometimes the fight between a protagonist and an antagonist is out in the open, and sometimes an antagonist uses sabotage to work behind the scenes.

- **Conflict with nature** *(person vs. nature).* Storms, high mountains, deserts, stinging insects…whatever gets in the protagonist's way or causes problems adds conflict, and the more the better.

   What if characters are ready to do battle just as a fierce blizzard descends? Swirling snow makes it impossible to see. What if a cloud of bats swarms around people lost in a cave? They might drop their flashlights and run, becoming even more lost. What if hikers venture too far into the desert without water? The blazing sun becomes an enemy. All this conflict is bad for the characters and good for the story.

- **Conflict with society** *(person vs. society).* Sometimes a character has a problem with customs or concepts of a culture or society. Maybe the society believes in stereotypes that try to force people into a "type"—as if everyone with red hair or dark skin or speaking with a particular accent must be the same. Characters struggling to be themselves despite stereotypes endure conflicts that can heighten the intensity in a story.

- **Conflict with machines** *(person vs. technology).* Machines can oppose people, either by attacking them or by subtly controlling their lives. There are now GPS chips the size of a speck of dust and lasers that can cut through steel. Computer surveillance can be set up in any home. Inventions move into daily life all the time. Technology can provide lots of conflict for a story.

- **The conflict of war** *(group vs. group).* A protagonist in a war zone will encounter heartache, injuries, death, and destruction. Individuals may be drawn into battles they don't want to fight. Groups may turn on each other. Nations once friendly may become foes. Warriors may pit their strength against one another. Some of the oldest written stories—such as the fall of Troy—are about war.

When conflict arises inside a character, it's called **internal conflict** *(person vs. self).* Here is an example of internal conflict that deals with struggling with feelings:

A girl's boyfriend breaks up with her. Then her best friend starts dating him. The girl has to admit to herself that her best friend and former boyfriend are perfect for each other, but she struggles with feelings of jealousy and loss.

Any intense upsetting emotion can grip a character—and whether the emotion is grief, worry, rage, bitterness, jealousy, fear, denial, etc., conflict mounts inside the person having those feelings.

Here are examples of internal conflict that deals with struggling with matters of conscience:

A boy who doesn't believe in lying can, by telling a lie, save his best friend from going to jail. What does he do?

Good stories are filled with conflict that begins early and ends late.

A girl's little sister needs glasses, but the family can't afford it. The girl finds two hundred dollars in a wallet lying in a grocery cart. Does she return the wallet or keep the money?

There are about a zillion possible ethical dilemmas, and characters can feel very conflicted about right and wrong.

Sometimes, stories combine both internal and external conflict. Imagine someone struggling with ethics while living in a war zone. Or a grief-stricken hero caught in a hurricane.

Looking for conflicts

Make an extended list of conflicts, including some that you've experienced yourself or observed in other people.

Could you put any of these conflicts into a story?

Annoyances. Not every source of friction in a story has to be an earth-shaking conflict. Daily annoyances also heighten tension. Here's an example by author Elise Leonard in which a character is woken from a pleasant dream:

> She gazed longingly through his thick eyeglass lenses with her beautiful cornflower blue eyes that saw no one and nothing else but him.
>
> The alarm buzzed, destroying the start of an obviously great dream.
>
> Perfect! Just when I finally fell asleep it was time to get up. I was tired, cranky, and wasn't looking forward to Mrs. Grenshaw's test.
>
> I shrugged into my red and blue plaid shirt, aligning the buttons, and brushed my teeth, reviewing the math formulas that would be covered on the exam. I knew them by heart so I didn't know why I was obsessing about them so much.
>
> Maybe because it was easier to think about math formulas than what was going on in this town.

Conflict can be internal or external.

Annoyances are embedded in Leonard's scene. Buttons, toothbrushes, math. Weariness. There's also a hint of larger problems "going on in this town." All of this grabs the attention.

COMPLICATIONS

Imagine that a character named Susannah has stayed up half the night finishing a major assignment. All that's left is printing it, which she decides to do in the morning. She falls into bed, sleeps until the alarm slices into her brain like a cleaver, and hurries to get ready for school. She tries to print her assignment, only to discover her printer ink cartridge is low and fails midway. She can't find her flash drive anywhere.

Susannah is encountering complications.

Or on the day of football tryouts, Dorian wakes up with a stuffy nose and streaming eyes. His throat aches and his lungs order him back to bed.

Now Dorian has complications.

Complications like these aren't drastic enough to make a good story because we've all experienced them in one form or another. But you could use these sorts of complications as a starting point with your characters, and then heap more hazards on their heads.

Suppose that Susannah not only has a problem finding her flash drive, but her computer crashes, destroying the original of her completed assignment. Her grade is hovering close to a D because she turns in so many assignments late. It so happens she was arrested four months ago for a third shoplifting offense. To keep from going to jail, she promised the prosecutor she would hold onto a C average.

Complications.

Or suppose that Dorian waited until the last day of football tryouts because he really wanted to perfect his pass. Sports are his life, but the coach is strict; if Dorian doesn't show up today, he won't get another chance unless he gets a doctor's note. He can't afford a doctor. If he can get to school and see the nurse on duty, he might be able to appease the coach, but when he staggers out of bed, his fever is so severe he wobbles, falls, and injures his throwing hand.

The best complications fit a character's nature. Let's say your main character drives a late model Lexus, loves designer clothes and jewelry, and enjoys flash-

Don't allow coincidence, chance, or a lucky break to come to your characters' rescue.

ing platinum credit cards around. If complications occur that take away the car, clothes, jewelry, and credit cards, the complication suits the character, causing tremendous pressure. But if a character is not materialistic, losing material things won't matter. For such a character, the loss of a friend will create far more tension than loss of a credit card.

Fitting Complications to Characters

In your mind, go over the plot of one of your favorite books. What complications do you find, and how do those complications fit the characters?

Building Your Story

Whether you've finished a story or you're partway through, look for complications. Do the complications fit the characters? Is there a hazard you've overlooked that could be heaped on someone's head?
Make any adjustments you feel are necessary.

Don't save your characters from conflict. Story complications should not be easy to resolve—if they are, tension gets deflated, like letting air out of balloons. Don't allow coincidence, chance, or a lucky break to come to your characters' rescue. Force characters to work things out on their own.

 MIDDLES AND ENDS

As conflict and complications exert pressure on characters, those characters take action. They push themselves and others.

They change.

As they change, they take more actions. Those actions lead to further complications, which lead to more pressure, which forces more action.

The best complications fit a character's nature.

Remember *in media res?* When the story starts, the life of your protagonist is in turmoil.

In the beginning of my book *The Seer and the Sword*, Prince Landen has lost everything he has except himself. He was born to peace and privilege but his homeland has been crushed by an invading force led by King Kareed of Archeld. Kareed kills Landen's father and takes the young prince captive. Landen finds himself in a foreign culture that values warrior training above all else. He has no fighting skills.

Conflict.

Actions follow. Landen learns to be a warrior.

Complications arise. He is hated and feared for his strength and his background. Another man kills the king and blames it on Landen.

Now we're in the middle of the story.

When one complication is resolved, it leads to another complication that's more intense and adds yet more conflict. Thus, when Landen leaves Archeld, his action saves his life, but new complications spring up.

The point is, throughout the middle, the pressure in your story is rising.

Climax. The climax takes place close to the end. It's the final culmination of all the conflicts. From the beginning, the conflict has been building, and at the climax it reaches its peak. It has to be resolved.

When you blow up a balloon, you add air pressure, stretching the balloon's skin until it's ready to pop. Same with stories. You keep adding pressure. By the time you hit the climax, the balloon must pop. Ka-bam!

The last chapter discussed the structure of plots as described in Christopher Booker's book, *The Seven Basic Plots*. Each basic plot has a different type of climax. The hero takes on the monster, the foe, or the ultimate test. A shadow is finally confronted, hidden natures are revealed, death and defeat move in, or the hero sees the light and finds redemption. (Booker 48–49, 83, 105–106, 150, 156–157, 204)

Don't cheat your readers. When you open up conflict early in a story, you are making a promise to your readers, a promise to stay with that conflict until it's resolved. If you meander away from it, readers will feel cheated.

Suppose J. R. R. Tolkien, author of *The Lord of the Rings*, had decided that halfway to Mount Doom, Frodo, the Hobbit—who is supposed to cast the Ring of Power into the fires of Mount Doom—should give up and go home? What if the One Ring turned out not to be dangerous after all? What if it turned out to be a quaint little item of magic and nothing more?

Deflated balloon. Readers would feel cheated.

Building Your Story

If you've finished a story of your own, look at the climax. What happens? Is it dramatic? Is the conflict resolved?

If you're partway through a story, think about the climax. What conflict opens up in the beginning? How will you resolve it?

Endings. Denouement—pronounced day-noo-MAH—is the term for how the story shakes out after the climax. It's the final outcome, the resolution that leads to the end. (For years I didn't look up the pronunciation of denouement and doubtless made a fool of myself by pronouncing it day-NOO-ment. Not only does it have a weird pronunciation, but it's also very hard to spell.)

In the denouement, you wrap up loose ends and finish the story. Frodo, the Hobbit, goes to live with the elves. Cinderella's stepsister, minus a big toe, limps to the wedding of Cinderella and the prince. Henry, the pilot, returns home to hug his father. Landen gets his kingdom back.

Getting through your whole story. Tom Clancy has a great quote about writing: "Success is a finished book, a stack of pages each of which is filled with words. If you reach that point, you have won a victory over yourself no less impressive than sailing single-handed around the world."

I agree. Getting from the beginning to the end of a story is a bold accomplishment. It's also more satisfying than your favorite food when you're hungry, your favorite friend when you're lonely, your favorite activity when you're full of energy—or all three at once.

So keep going. Don't get derailed. If you've reached the middle, you can get to the end.

Your creative mind and intuition got you into the story. Let them bring you through it. If, like me, you feel like you're tunneling through solid rock on your first draft, that's okay. If you feel as if you're swimming underwater during a storm,

The climax of a story is the final culmination of all the conflicts.

that's fine too. If it seems an earthquake has taken hold, shaking the ground you thought was solid, don't worry about it.

If you keep going, you'll get through the rock. You'll make it to the surface of the water. The ground will quit trembling. And you'll have your story.

Getting from the beginning to the end of a story is a bold accomplishment.

POLISHING YOUR WRITING

CHAPTER TEN

POLISHING YOUR WRITING

**There are three rules for writing.
Unfortunately, no one can agree what they are.**
— Somerset Maugham

The pen is mightier than the sword.
— Edward Bulwer-Lytton

Authors often seek out other writers and ask for criticism, or *critique* as it's called. This is because you cannot objectively read your own work for the first time. It's not possible. So you ask trustworthy readers to point out plot holes or cardboard characters or stilted dialogue you may have missed. Trust me—even very experienced writers still need this sort of help.

Taking criticism. It takes practice to get used to sorting through criticism for the parts that will be helpful. Some writers are defensive at first and have trouble accepting even a friendly critique. But eventually you learn not only to accept but even to relish criticism. If someone finds a gaping hole in your plot or notices a character who seems to have no life, listening to criticism will make all the difference.

Helpful critiques. Critiques that are full of specifics can be quite helpful. Here are some hypothetical examples:

> On page 37, when Ava agrees to meet Doug after school, why doesn't she tell her best friend Greta that she won't be on the bus?

In Chapter Two, why do Lindsay and Charlie get together? I don't understand what they see in each other.

On page 25, when Van punches Luke as he's riding past on his bike, wouldn't he lose his balance and crash?

If you find you truly love writing, you might try seeking out people who can give you helpful critiques. Sometimes schools or libraries have creative writing groups that meet on a regular basis. If you can't find a group, you might start one yourself. There's nothing like making friends for life while improving your writing by leaps and bounds.

Unhelpful critiques. Scornful comments don't help you improve. "Ava is stupid." "This is the worst thing I've ever read." "What made you think you could write a story?"

The downside of sharing your writing is that once you put it out there, you can't take it back. You're likely to remember the reactions you get. If comments are insulting, they can really hurt.

Classroom critiques. School classrooms have variables beyond your control.

Sometimes you get an outstanding teacher and a group of students who set a supportive atmosphere. Under those conditions, sharing your writing can boost your inspiration and help you grow as a writer much faster than you could on your own.

On the other hand, sometimes you find yourself in a class where the teacher doles out harsh criticism or some of the students like to sneer. In a situation like that, there's no reason to risk sharing a piece of writing that reveals your innermost thoughts and feelings. In such a case, if you get an assignment to write a story that will be shared with the class, write about something that doesn't much matter to you. Save the stories that are close to your heart for other times and places.

Use your judgment. I recommend using your judgment when choosing which stories you'll share and with whom. Test new situations. Notice how people are treating each other. Are they respectful? Are they kind? Do they say helpful things? Or do they rip each other to shreds?

It's excruciating to pour your heart and soul into a story and then get slammed.

Your story belongs to you.

But it's exhilarating and motivating to find people who truly care about your characters and know how to give a helpful critique. Meeting with such people can bring excitement to the practice of writing.

It's always your call. Your story belongs to you. Weigh carefully everything other people tell you about what you've written. Sometimes critiques are excellent, but sometimes they miss the mark. You get to decide which parts of your story you'll keep and which you'll jettison. You get to choose whether to develop a new plot line or stick with what you have. It's your call.

You, and only you, are the author.

POLISHING, POLISHING

Learning ways to critique your own work can be quite enjoyable—at least I think so. For one thing, understanding how to write clearly helps a writer feel more confident.

The following tips offer a few techniques on style. (No accident that the word *style* comes from *stylus*, a writing instrument used by ancient people to etch words into wax tablets.) You can use them to edit yourself when you're ready.

Words. It's your words that get your readers to feel what you want them to feel. When I go through my story drafts for the second or third (or fourth or fifth) time, one of the things I'm looking for is how my nouns, verbs, and adjectives are shaping up. As Mark Twain said, "The difference between the right word and the wrong word is the difference between lightning and a lightning bug."

The word *arachnid* rather than *spider* brings a whole different feeling to a paragraph. *Violet* really is different from *purple*. *Confounded* gives a slightly different meaning than *bewildered*.

What's the difference between these words?

look	scrutinize
try	venture
fear	horror
bad food	obnoxious glop
complete nonsense	unmitigated drivel

Finding the word you really want is a joyous thing.

plain purse	ugly tote
nice rays	luscious sunshine

Sometimes the short words are better, and sometimes the long ones are. Finding the word you really want—the one that gets across what you're after—is a joyous thing.

Verbs are said to be strong when they don't need the help of an adjective or adverb. Here are some examples:

Verb plus adverb: *took immediately* Strong verb: *seized*
Verb plus adjective: *closed hard*   Strong verb: *slammed*
Verb plus adverb and adjective: *ate very fast* Strong verb: *devoured*
Verb plus two adverbs: *moved along rapidly* Strong verb: *hurried*

By strengthening your verbs, you can give your story a feeling of intense action.

Experimenting With Verbs

Using the list of weak verbs and modifers on the left above, write a short scene.
Now substitute the strong verbs for the weak ones.
What happens to your scene?

De-cluttering. Another all-important thing to look for when polishing a story is cluttered sentences. Like cluttered rooms, they're seldom appreciated.

It's easy to know what makes a room cluttered: disorganized piles of laundry, dirty dishes, crumpled empty bags of snacks, etc.

But what makes a cluttered sentence?

One culprit is redundancy. In daily speech, we're redundant all the time, but writing sounds cleaner without redundancy. In these examples, the redundant word is in italics, followed by the sentence without the redundancy.

She stood *up*.	She stood.
He sat *down*.	He sat.

By strengthening your verbs, you can give your story a feeling of intense action.

They climbed *up* the slope.	They climbed the slope.
The boy followed *along with them*.	The boy followed.
She *looked and* saw a chicken.	She saw a chicken.

Redundancy can be more than a word or phrase. It can afflict a whole sentence and then spread to a paragraph. Here's an example of a paragraph cluttered with redundancy:

Many more arrows whizzed around them, making frightening sounds in the air. One of the arrows struck Fahd in the chest, but the arrow didn't hurt him. It bounced off the thick hide of his striped doublet and landed on the ground without doing any damage.

Here's the same paragraph, without the redundancies:

More arrows whizzed around them. One struck Fahd in the chest but bounced off the thick hide of his striped doublet.

Unnecessary words and phrases also clutter sentences.

Cluttered:

A person who has never made a single mistake when trying to get something done is a person who has never really made the attempt upon something he or she hasn't tried to do before.

Uncluttered:

Anyone who has never made a mistake has never tried anything new. (Albert Einstein)

Cluttered:

Sara used the rake like a broom in order to sweep fragrant grass clippings and get them into a heap. Then when she was finished, she put away the rake.

Uncluttered:

Sara used the rake like a broom to sweep fragrant grass clippings into a heap. When she finished, she put away the rake.

Unnecessary words and phrases clutter sentences.

Cluttered:

The many writing techniques that you have been instructed about can be likened to the special precision machines that can cut the separate facets of raw gemstones, thereby bringing out the stones' ability to sparkle.

Uncluttered:

Writing techniques are like the precision machines that cut gemstones to bring out their sparkle.

Building Your Story

When you're in a good mood, take a look at all of the pages you've written on your story so far. Search out redundancies and unnecessary words. When you find them, circle them. Then set the story aside. Come back to it later and rewrite.

Passive voice. In writing fiction, use passive voice with care. Wondering what "passive voice" is? It's when the subject of the sentence receives the action of the verb rather than taking the action. Here are some examples:

Passive:

Her suitcase was shoved in the backseat. The wheel was taken by the woman.

Active:

The woman shoved her suitcase in the backseat. She took the wheel.

Passive:

The computer was turned on, and paper was stocked in the printer.

Active:

He turned on the computer and stocked the printer with paper.

Passive:

The arrow was shot from the bow and the target was hit right in the bullseye.

Active:

The arrow flew, hitting the bullseye.

Writing in active voice is usually much stronger.

Cadence. What is cadence? It's the rhythm and flow behind the words we write. If you read sentences aloud, and imagine that they have a beat, such as "DA da-da DA" or "da-da da-da DA-da" you'll get a sense of cadence.

Here's a short paragraph in which the sentences all have a similar cadence:

Joe bought a sandwich. Joe ate his sandwich. Joe didn't like it.

That's an exaggerated example, just for effect. But it really is a problem when a paragraph has sentence after sentence with a similar rhythm, similar number of syllables, and similar style. Such writing can lull a reader to sleep.

To show more about cadence, I've borrowed a paragraph from author James Van Pelt, a well-written paragraph in which the cadence changes. Van Pelt has short sentences and long ones. The longer sentences have different rhythms. Try reading the paragraph aloud, paying attention to the beat of each sentence.

Clarence remembered running home down the long muddy lane beside the field, its corn already harvested, the broken stalks lying across each other. He'd run on the weeds beside the lane to keep his shoes dry. Then he stumbled. For a second, he thought he'd stepped in the mud, but he could see the shoe was clean. His right leg dragged again. He slowed to a heavy limp, massaging his thigh through his jeans. What was wrong with his leg? The house had never looked so far away. Too far to call for help. He leaned on the fence and felt his strength fading.

Below, I've mangled Van Pelt's wonderful paragraph. If you read what I've done aloud, you'll notice I've forced the sentences to have a similar cadence, destroying the flow of the writing:

Use passive voice with care.

Clarence remembered running home down the muddy lane. The field's corn had been harvested into broken stalks. Clarence ran on the weeds beside the lane to keep dry. He stumbled and thought he'd stepped in mud. He could see the shoe was clean but his right leg dragged. He slowed to a heavy limp, massaging his thigh. There must be something wrong with his leg or it wouldn't drag. The house had never looked so far away. He leaned on the fence and tried to rest.

If you want your readers to stay awake, vary your cadence.

Bad writing to get good. Sometimes it's helpful to do the opposite of what you know you should do, first. I sometimes write badly on purpose, stringing adjectives into long streamers and sprinkling adverbs like confetti. It's a way to remind myself I don't have to follow the rules of good writing every single minute. I can let the careless writer in me run wild, and once in a while she comes up with something worth keeping.

Overwriting, like overacting, can show you how much is too much, as in this example describing a fantasy character.

Overwritten:

Beside Fahd, Maeve appeared extremely delicate and unbelievably small. She was totally ragged and unkempt, while Fahd's doublet gleamed with a shining coat of freshly-applied oil. Maeve had no knowledge of how to use any weapons, so she had none, but Fahd's sharp black axe and glimmering silver knife hung at his belt at all times. Jasper would have bet everything he ever hoped to have in this life on Maeve's unusual and extraordinary brand of courage, but outwardly she was hardly the picture of someone who could command a rugged band of hard-bitten warriors.

Now here's the same description after trimming:

Beside Fahd, Maeve appeared delicate—small, ragged and weapon-less. Jasper would have bet his life on Maeve's courage, but outwardly she was hardly the picture of someone in command of warriors.

Most writers go through many drafts before getting one they like. There are a lot of ways to approaching rewriting, probably as many ways as there are writers.

Some people go full speed through a first draft and don't even try to make it any good. Then they go back and start from the beginning with a second draft, and work through that quickly, too. Maybe they slow down for the third draft. Others write a chapter in the evening and then revise that same chapter in the morning. Still others go through every draft with meticulous care.

Personally, I throw as much onto the page as I can stand to put there, and then read it over when I want to take a break from the hard labor of a first draft. It's always easier for me to polish something that's already there than to come up with something from nothing. In fact, I absolutely love the process of polishing. But I've talked with writers who dread revisions as much as I dread a first draft.

You are you. Experiment until you find what works.

If it gets you there, it gets you there.

Overwriting and Trimming

Write a scene or a character description, letting yourself go wild with adjectives and adverbs. After you're done, trim the excess.
You might be surprised by how much you like what's left.

Most writers go through many drafts before getting one they like.

POINT OF VIEW

CHAPTER ELEVEN

POINT OF VIEW

My aim is to put down on paper what I feel and what I see in the best and simplest way.
— Ernest Hemingway

All the fun is in how you say a thing.
— Robert Frost

You've arrived at the last chapter about technique. Congratulations!

Now you get to think about what point of view you'll use to write your story. First person (I)? Second person (you)? Third person (he/she/they)?

"Point of view" means different things in different contexts. To look at the world from someone else's "point of view" is one meaning—and it's the one everybody is used to. But now we're going to delve into definitions of *literary* point of view. (By the way, this is considered advanced territory on the writing journey, so if you need to go over this chapter more than once or twice, you're normal.) As you'll soon understand, literary point of view (POV) can be the same for many characters, because it's about the way a writer writes the story. It's the underlying structure.

Let me explain.

FIRST PERSON POV

One common point of view is first person. In first person, the story is viewed through the senses and mind of an "I" character. Books written in first person include *To Kill a Mockingbird* (Harper Lee), *Thirteen* (Lauren Myracle), and *Twilight* (Stephenie Meyer).

Here are some examples of first person POV:

> The sun was so hot and my skin so bumpy, I felt like a bag of chili peppers fire-roasted in an outdoor oven.

> I hate the dark more than I hate scorpions, spiders, and stingrays combined.

> I opened the envelope with one quick slice of my thumb. I skimmed the first paragraph and then tried to keep my lips from trembling.
> "Well?" Kelly asked. "Did you get accepted?"
> I shook my head. "Not this year."

Notice how the "I" character changes from one example to the next, but the point of view stays the same. It's always first person. All "I" characters reveal their personalities and perspective by what they say and how they say it.

"I" characters can talk about other characters, as they do here:

> Dag has the world's worst acne, but his eyes are as clear as a good day at the beach. The acne will go away eventually, so I focus on his eyes.

> Poor Inga can't walk past a boy without hunching her shoulders and staring at the floor. She has the lowest self-esteem of any of my friends.

> My sister sticks her nose into anything she gets halfway near. I wouldn't let her within fifty feet of my journal, which is why I have to go to the trouble of taking it with me wherever I go. Yesterday I left my backpack near the doorway. The minute she got home she started digging through it. I sprinted down the stairs and tackled her. "Stay away from my stuff!" I yelled. She acted like it was my fault she got a bruise on her shoulder. Unbelievable.

Advantages of first person POV. With first person POV, the "I" character can easily reveal anything he or she experiences, including thoughts and feelings. This can lead to a feeling of closeness with the character.

In first person, the story is viewed through the senses and mind of an "I" character.

Disadvantages of first person. When you write in first person, you can't write anything your "I" character doesn't experience. So you can't use "meanwhile, back at the zoo" or "meanwhile back at the rodeo" to show what happened somewhere else; scenes letting readers know what people are doing in two different places aren't allowed. This is a disadvantage when you want to show what's going on with people the first person character can't see.

For example, let's say you have two characters named Trina and Leo, and Trina spends the day searching for Leo, who has gone cave-diving without telling her. It would be handy to be able to say *And while Trina searched desperately for Leo, he spent the day cave-diving, out of touch with everything else.* But if Trina is a first person character, you would have to write about her search for Leo differently: *I searched desperately for Leo, but he was nowhere to be found.*

If the first person character doesn't see something happening, the only way to find out about it is by talking with people who were there or finding evidence somehow, as in the following examples:

> After I searched desperately for Leo all day long, he finally called and told me he'd been cave-diving, out of touch with the world.

> I snuck into Leo's room and searched his closet. His cave-diving equipment was missing. He must have decided to go off to the caves alone without telling me.

If the "I" character is running toward a dark corner where an angry thug is waiting, you can't let the reader know about the angry thug before the first person character gets there. You can only say *I ran toward the dark corner*—or something similar. (There is an exception. If your "I" character is looking back in time, he or she can say, *As I ran toward the dark corner that day, I didn't know an angry thug was lurking in the shadows ready to pounce.*)

Writing in First Person

Imagine a character. Using first person POV, write a paragraph that tells the reader important things about who the character is.

When you write in first person, you can't write anything your "I" character doesn't experience.

SECOND PERSON POV

In second person, the story is viewed through the senses and mind of a "you" character. If you've ever read a *Choose Your Own Adventure* book (R. A. Montgomery), you've seen second person POV.

Here are some examples of second person POV:

> As you try to get next to one of the girls at the dance, you start to wheeze. Evidently, one can of hairspray wasn't enough for her! You swear you're going to pass out from the fumes. "I'm getting out of here," you mutter, and back away.

> You walk along the beach and see dead fish lying along the sand. Seagulls are screaming at the fish as if they want to wake them up.

Second person is almost always written in present tense.

Advantages of second person POV. An advantage of second person is that the tone is informal. Also, the combination of the informal "you" and the present tense can give a sense of motion to the story, as if you are telling a friend about it as you walk down the street.

Disadvantages of second person POV. Second person is rarely used and takes concentration to maintain. It's much easier to speak in second person than to write in it.

Writing in Second Person

Take the paragraph you wrote in first person, and convert it to second person. See if anything more occurs to you to say when writing in this POV.

An advantage of second person is that the tone is informal. Second person is rarely used and takes concentration to maintain.

THIRD PERSON POV

In third person, a narrator tells the story, using "he," "she," and sometimes "they" to talk about the characters.

There are several divisions of third person POV, but we're only going to cover the two most common versions, which are *limited third person* and *omniscient.*

Limited third person POV. In the most common type of limited third person, the story is viewed through the mind and senses of one "he" or "she" character. Nancy Farmer's book *The Sea of Trolls* is written in limited third person. So is Bruce Coville's *Jeremy Thatcher, Dragon Hatcher.*

In limited third person, the author can write the same information that's in first person by switching "I" to "he" or "she." Here's an example:

First person:

> I felt sick to my stomach all of a sudden. Without warning, I threw up the lake water I'd drunk. It spewed out of my mouth as if I'd been rigged as a fountain. To my horror, some of it splattered on Daniel.
>
> "Oh, no," I moaned. What would he think of me now?

The same selection, rewritten in third person:

> Amber felt sick to her stomach all of a sudden. Without warning, she threw up the lake water she'd drunk. It spewed out of her mouth as if she'd been rigged as a fountain. To her horror, some of it splattered on Daniel.
>
> "Oh, no," she moaned. What would he think of her now?

The same information is there each time, but it lands in the reader's mind a little differently. The tone of third person isn't as confiding as the tone of first person, so there's more separation between the reader and the main character.

When writing in limited third person, much depends on the character you choose for "he" or "she" because that character's perspective will decide how the story unfolds. To show what I mean, here's an example of the same scene written from the perspective of three different characters.

Evan's perspective:

Evan's stomach was a pit of misery, crying for food. The small skylight showed that day was near gone, but he and the other boys had not been fed. No sign of Boz for hours. Were they meant to starve here?

The boy called Wolf charged the door again and again, pounding on it, shouting through bruised lips. Evan wished Wolf would bide his time, watch and find out all he could. That was what Evan planned to do.

Wolf's perspective:

The glow from the skylight was getting dim, and still no one had brought any food. Wolf's stomach felt like an empty pit. How dare Boz keep them here? How dare he?

Hunger and fury built in Wolf's heart and coursed through his body. He rushed at the door and slammed himself against it. He raised his fists and pounded.

"Let us out!" he yelled, beating the senseless wood harder and harder.

Boz's perspective:

Boz heard pounding from the holding room. He glanced out his window. The sun was ready to sink, and the boys must be getting hungry. Who among them had disobeyed his orders? What fool was beating on the door, a door made of oak harder than iron? He'd lay odds it was Wolf. The young man didn't know when to give up.

Although all three perspectives are written from limited third person, each has a different focus according to the personality of the "he" character viewing the scene. Evan has the perspective of a captive who hopes to avoid drawing attention to himself so he can plan an escape. Wolf has the perspective of an angry and reckless young man ready to fight for his freedom. Boz has the attitude of a cruel warden.

Which perspective do you think does the best job of showing what's going on?

In third person, a narrator tells the story, using "he," "she," and sometimes "they" to talk about the characters.

Advantages of limited third person POV. With limited third person POV, you can get close to the protagonist and reveal his or her thoughts and feelings. But because the style of writing is less confiding, it doesn't feel so centrally focused on one character's internal life the way it would in first person.

Disadvantages of limited third person POV. When you write in this type of limited third person, you can't write about anything the "he/she" character doesn't experience.

Writing Different Perspectives in Limited Third Person

Imagine a short scene. Write the same scene from three different limited third person perspectives.

What do you notice about the variety of details you bring out in each scene?

Third person omniscient POV. In third person omniscient point of view, the narrator is all-knowing and is therefore never limited to what any particular character can experience. (For this reason, omniscient POV is also known as "unlimited.")

The narrator can choose to describe what anyone in the story is doing, feeling, thinking, or looking like, at any time, anywhere. The narrator can describe events from long ago or far in the future. The narrator can even describe what's happening in scenes when characters are not present, for example a lonely flower in a desert, a tidal wave beginning deep in the ocean, or a fire starting from a lightning strike in a remote forest.

Books written from omniscient point of view include *The Lord of the Rings* (J. R. R. Tolkien), *Inkheart* (Cornelia Funke), *A Wizard of Earthsea* (Ursula K. LeGuin), and many, many more.

In omniscient view, it's the narrator's choice how much to reveal. There's a wide scope for storytelling, and plenty of choices open to the author. The main thing to remember about this point of view is that the narrator knows everything—whether he or she chooses to reveal everything or not.

In the following example of third person omniscient POV, the narrator observes three different characters' thoughts and feelings:

In omniscient view, it's the narrator's choice how much to reveal.

Uncle John stirred uneasily in his recliner as Janey slipped out the door. That girl certainly got some peculiar notions in her head. Did she really believe the new man in town was a rainmaker—whatever that was? At eighteen, shouldn't she have more sense?

Janey didn't even pause to put on a raincoat or grab an umbrella. She dashed across the street to where Darvis stood at the curbside, his head tilted as if listening to the sky.

When his strange watery eyes fell on her, Janey gulped and looked away, up into the vast gray cloud above. Water patted her skin softly, water from heaven. Why had she never noticed before how wonderful it was?

Darvis beamed at the young woman who seemed unafraid of getting soaked. Could it be he had finally found a person who could understand the beauty of the cloud he had brought with him?

Another example, focusing on a scene at the seashore, written in third person omniscient POV:

The three boys raced each other down the sand toward the ocean, but as they neared the water's edge, they forgot about who was running faster. They became aware of an overpowering smell—rotten and fishy. They stopped and stared at the row of dead fish lining the shore. Seagulls screamed overhead, wheeling in frantic circles as if sounding an alarm. Desperate to get away, the boys turned and sprinted back the way they had come. After they left, the beach was deserted for the rest of the afternoon. Only the seagulls watched as the waves washed in and out with a slushy, dispirited sound, as if the water knew something was wrong.

Because omniscient POV is so unlimited, authors choose to use it in many different ways. Some focus more on one of their characters than the others. Some focus on several primary characters more or less equally. Some move freely through the heads and hearts of any character on the scene, whether that character is primary or secondary. And some spend a fair amount of time describing what's happening with volcanoes, hurricanes, forest fires, or other natural phenomena. It's the author's decision what to reveal and whose perspective to emphasize.

In omniscient POV, there is great freedom.

Advantages of third person omniscient POV. In first person, second person, and limited third person, there are limits built in to the POV. But in omniscient POV, there is great freedom. Any limits are chosen by the writer. The main challenge becomes how much to leave out and what your focus will be.

Disadvantages of third person omniscient POV. Omniscient view creates an effect of looking out over the story. Because of this, readers may not feel quite as close to individual characters.

Other points of view. People who study literary points of view in depth have terms for more categories and subcategories of POV than those I've outlined in this chapter. However, it's not necessary to learn every term and category to write a great story, and you have plenty of information here to get started.

Writing in Omniscient POV

Decide on a scene you want to write. What is the focus of the scene? Write it from an all-knowing point of view. Let the reader know what's going on without giving too much away.

Practicing Point of View

Pick a favorite passage from a novel. Rewrite it in various viewpoints. If it's in first person, rewrite it in limited third. Try an omniscient point of view, or even second person. Experiment.

CHOOSING YOUR POV

Choosing a point of view for your story is a big decision. Since everything is filtered through POV, your choice will determine how the characters and action will unfold.

As you practice different points of view, you'll find that certain types are much more natural to you. When you find the POV that's right for a story, you'll feel as if the story is more *there*. Your characters will be eager to let you know what's going on with them. They may wake you up at night, smile at you when you least expect it, whisper in your creative ear urging you to get on with your writing.

You might be surprised by which POV you like best. Maybe you've assumed you should write in third person when in fact first person is what brings out your voice the best for many stories. Maybe you've always written first person but when you switch to omniscient, your characters go bounding onto the page. Or maybe you like second person best for one story, and omniscient for another.

Finding the POV that fits is such an important discovery, it's worth experimenting.

Building Your Story

Write a scene from your own story in first person.

Just for fun, rewrite it in second. Then rewrite it in limited third person. Then omniscient third person, revealing whatever you wish

Each time, check to see what it's like for you as a writer. Is there a certain point of view that feels clogged and stiff when you're writing? Is there another point of view where your words pour out more easily?

INTO THE FUTURE

CHAPTER TWELVE

INTO THE FUTURE

**Hold fast to dreams for if dreams die,
life is a broken-winged bird that cannot fly.**
— Langston Hughes

If you've made it this far, you must be a writer at heart. Why else would you go through all those chapters about dialogue brackets, plot lines, and *in media res?* Those are not subjects just anyone would choose to read about. The fact that you've done so says a lot about you.

On your writing journey, you've probably been advised to practice your skills—and it's true that practice has an important place. Professional musicians put in more time rehearsing than performing. Marathon runners start with a few laps and go up from there, training hard. Pop stars spend a gazillion hours practicing how to look sexy while sweating.

What pushes musicians and pop stars to practice so much? Why do marathon runners keep going mile after mile? And why would a writer bother with one draft after another?

Passion.

By reading this entire book, you've proved that your passion for writing goes deep. There's an artist within you who looks at the world through the strangely glowing lens of a storyteller. I hope your passion continues to inspire you to write more and more, learn all you can, and freewrite daily.

INTERVIEWS WITH AUTHORS

CHAPTER THIRTEEN

INTERVIEWS WITH AUTHORS

I'm not afraid of storms, for I'm learning how to sail my ship.
—Louisa May Alcott

Fiction is the truth inside the lie.
—Stephen King

Next in *Seize the Story* is a collection of interviews with published authors, people with a passion for writing. All of them describe a little about their own unique approaches, and give advice for teens like you—teens who want to write fiction. Enjoy!

T. A. Barron.............................134

Joan Bauer 136

Hilari Bell.................................139

Dia Calhoun.............................142

Chris Crutcher.........................143

Teresa R. Funke 145

Nancy Garden 147

Elise Leonard 149

David Lubar 152

Carolyn Meyer.........................154

Todd Mitchell...........................156

Lauren Myracle........................158

Donita K. Paul.........................160

Stephanie Perkins.....................162

Laura Resau 164

Olugbemisola
Rhuday-Perkovich....................166

Lynda Sandoval........................168

James Van Pelt 169

Denise Vega 172

Q&A

T. A. BARRON
http://www.tabarron.com

Published books (complete list on website)
The Great Tree of Avalon trilogy:
>   *Child of the Dark Prophecy*
>   *Shadows on the Stars*
>   *The Eternal Flame*

The Lost Years of Merlin epic:
>   *The Lost Years of Merlin*
>   *The Seven Songs of Merlin*
>   *The Fires of Merlin*
>   *The Mirror of Merlin*
>   *The Wings of Merlin*

The Adventures of Kate trilogy:
>   *Heartlight*
>   *The Ancient One*
>   *The Merlin Effect*

Merlin's Dragon trilogy:
>   *Merlin's Dragon*
>   *Doomraga's Revenge*
>   *Ultimate Magic*

What do you find to be the easiest thing about writing?

Very little about writing is easy! But it's a remarkably clarifying experience. Writing is more than a craft: It is a way of life. One of the best aspects of writing is that it allows me to experience, to explore, anything I want. As a writer I can find the voice

of a twelve-year-old girl, be an ancient stone, or become a young wizard. I can experience life in the most wondrous ways. If I'm lucky enough to find a character who has lots of richness and depth, such as Merlin, then as the character grows, so do I. And, I hope, so do readers.

What do you find to be the hardest thing about writing?

The hardest part is the discipline to keep writing when I'd rather be wrestling with my kids, baking cookies, going for a hike, or having more time with my wife. Writing is the hardest labor I know—but it is also, if you stay with it, the most joyous labor of all.

What's your best advice for teens who want to write fiction?

My advice for teens who want to write boils down to three words: Observe. Practice. Believe.

OBSERVE the world around you—in deep, sensuous detail.

PRACTICE writing every chance you get! Write letters, poems, stories, plays, even fortune cookies—but write.

BELIEVE—in yourself and also in your story. Always remember you have something valuable to say.

JOAN BAUER
http://www.joanbauer.com

Published books
Squashed
Thwonk
Sticks
Rules of the Road
Backwater
Hope Was Here
Stand Tall
Best Foot Forward
Peeled
Close to Famous

What do you find to be the easiest thing about writing?

Writing dialogue, probably. I was trained as a screenwriter and learned how to tell a story through conversation. I do hear the book in my head when the writing is going well. I can hear the main character talking, sense the pacing, the nuances in language, voice, and conversation. Also, I do find humorous moments much easier to write than serious ones.

What do you find to be the hardest thing about writing?

Description! I can hear my characters, but I just can't see them unless they have some distinctive feature, like being hugely tall (Tree in *Stand Tall*) or being slightly overweight (Ellie in *Squashed*). I've often said I have taken an emotional X-ray of

my characters and I know their hearts and minds so well, but describing them is difficult. Part of this is because it doesn't matter to me what they look like as much as who they are inside. My editor is always asking me to provide more description, and sometimes I'll get photos in magazines of normal people and describe them in my stories. Ah, now my dark secret is out.

What's your best advice for teens who want to write humor into their fiction?

First, I think you can overthink humor and talk yourself out of being funny. So if it's possible, just let something flow. For example, you can start by having a character who has one quirky, funny characteristic, like talking to his fish. In all other ways, this is a regular kid, but the fish talking comes up at unusual moments, and that's really funny.

Surprise is a big part in humor; so is anticipating that something is going to be funny. In the case of the guy who talks to his fish, anticipation could come when his girlfriend comes over and he's trying to impress her, and we see that his fish is in the aquarium in the room. The girl goes over to it and the guy is trying to hold back, but he just can't do it. The reader is waiting for him to do something agonizingly odd, and that in itself is funny. The payoff (the big joke) comes when the guy talks to the fish and the girl looks at him like he's crazy.

I think, too, that humor shouldn't be separate from other things—it should be in drama, in tragedy, in fantasy, etc. One of the things people often say after they've come through a very hard time is, "I can remember when I began to laugh again." Remembering how humor can lift us up from difficult moments is another way to use it. Usually, when I'm telling a serious part of a story, in the next chapter or scene I'll introduce something funny.

When I wrote *Rules of the Road,* which is at its core the story of a girl trying to deal with her alcoholic father, the father shows up at the shoe store where Jenna works. He's drunk, and it's humiliating to her. It's a tough scene, but I made it funny by using broad comedy. A helium tank is in the back of the shoe store,

and Jenna—kidding around—takes a suck of the gas. Her voice gets high and funny and that's the moment her dad comes into the store.

The other way to think about writing humor is to keep a file of the things that make you laugh. Generally, my rule is, if something makes me laugh, it will make others laugh.

One more thought—the best humor tends to be short. It's possible to have too much build-up and you lose the laugh. I also don't care for mean-spirited humor. I think the power of humor is when it cuts through a situation and brings clarity. William Zinsser said, "What I want to do is to make people laugh so that they'll see things clearly."

Author Q & A

HILARI BELL
http://www.sfwa.org/members/bell

Published books
Songs of Power
Navohar (a book for adults)
A Matter of Profit
The Goblin Wood
The Goblin Gate
The Goblin War
The Wizard Test
The Prophecy
Farsala trilogy:
    Fall of a Kingdom
    Rise of a Hero
    Forging the Sword
Shield, Sword & Crown:
    Shield of Stars
    Sword of Waters
    Crown of Earth
    The Last Knight
    Rogue's Home
    Player's Ruse
Trickster's Girl
Traitor's Son (2012)

What do you find to be the easiest thing about writing?
I'm not sure there's anything about writing that's really easy. Fun, absolutely. I love most aspects of writing, and even

the nit-picky work of going over a copy edit is interesting. (The last one finally forced me to learn how to properly use "was/were" after an "if"—because sometimes the copy editor was getting it wrong!) But even plotting out a story, which is the part of the process I enjoy most, isn't what I'd call easy. Fascinating, enthralling, and loads of fun, but it also entails a lot of hard thinking.

What do you find to be the hardest thing about writing?

The hardest thing about writing, I think, is figuring out how to change a story when I already have it down on paper. Even when I know that there's something missing from the middle third, and that my writers' group was absolutely right when they told me to add a murder and a subplot, breaking into the flow of my established prose to add the necessary scenes—and cutting all the stuff that suddenly became unnecessary—is pretty tough.

In fact, for me each successive draft is a little less fun and a little more work than the one before it. I blast through the first draft with tons of energy and creative fire. The second draft, where I find and correct everything I can see that's wrong with the manuscript is less fun, but the story is still alive and improving.

The next two drafts are the ones described above, where I'm incorporating suggestions first from my writers' group, and then from my editor, and they're tougher. Then comes the editorial line edit, where the editor is nit-picking sentences and paragraphs. That's even more tedious, but at least there's living voice to work with.

Then finally the copy edit, where yet another editor nitpicks my punctuation and grammar—and also catches mistakes that make me cringe, like when someone becomes a year younger between one chapter and the next. I really do appreciate my copy editors almost all the time, but this draft feels like trying to animate a corpse. There's a lot about writing that's hard, when you come down to it.

What's your best advice for teens who want to write fiction?

Read lots. Written English is a different dialect than spoken English—same vocabulary, but different syntax and different rhythms. If you've ever read a story written by someone who really does write the way people talk, then you know what I mean. If you train your writer's "ear" until written English comes to you naturally, you give yourself a huge advantage. Of course, if you start talking in written English you run the risk of having people ask if you're British or Greek. (When I was a kid people asked me if I was British all the time—Greek only happened once.) But after a while you'll get used to telling them that, no, you were born and raised in Colorado—you're just speaking in written English. And when they look funny at you—and they do!—you just smile and tell yourself that someday you'll be a writer.

DIA CALHOUN
http://www.diacalhoun.com

Published books
The Return of Light: A Christmas Tale
Avielle of Rhia
The Phoenix Dance
White Midnight
Aria of the Sea
Firegold

What do you find to be the easiest thing about writing?

For me, the easiest thing about writing is word-tinkering. I love playing with language, playing with words and sentences. Revising is a joy because of this. I can get lost in a paragraph for hours at a time, trying it one way and then another, reading it out loud. This is why I am a writer.

What do you find to be the hardest thing about writing?

Plotting is definitely the most difficult part of writing for me.

What's your best advice for teens who want to write fiction?

Read, read, read! Read everything you can, as broadly as you can. Also, try to write a little bit every day. I find if I write every day, my subconscious mind does an enormous amount of the work for me. Ideas keep percolating. And finally, *finish* something, a story or novel or poem. There is so much to be learned from completing a piece of work.

Author Q & A

CHRIS CRUTCHER

http://www.chriscrutcher.com

Published books
Running Loose
Stotan!
The Crazy Horse Electric Game
Chinese Handcuffs
Athletic Shorts
The Deep End
Staying Fat for Sarah Byrnes
Ironman
Whale Talk
King of the Mild Frontier
The Sledding Hill
Deadline
Angry Management

What do you find to be the easiest thing about writing?

The easiest thing for me is writing dialogue and action. I've got a good ear for story, so those things are easiest and they tend to keep me focused. It's a good idea to always lead with your strength.

What do you find to be the hardest thing about writing?

The hardest thing for me is getting started and describing things. I don't "see" as well as I "hear," so descriptions

are difficult for me. Also, I'm the biggest procrastinator ever created.

What's your best advice for teens who want to write fiction?

Read as much of the kind of fiction you want to write, and write every day. If something makes you laugh, write it down. If something makes you angry, write it down. If something disappoints you or makes you sad, write it down. Writing is like working out. The more you do it the better you get.

TERESA R. FUNKE
http://www.teresafunke.com

Published books
Remember Wake
Dancing in Combat Boots
Doing My Part
The No-No Boys
V for Victory

What do you find to be the easiest thing about writing?

It's always easy to do something you love. So the easiest thing for me is just doing it! I've wanted to be a writer since I was ten years old, and any time I had a writing assignment or book report, I was happy. Writing well (which includes lots of rewriting) is a challenge, and I like a good challenge.

What do you find to be the hardest thing about writing?

Coming up with ideas that work is hardest for me. At times the ideas won't come at all. Other times, I start working on a story or essay only to realize my idea isn't strong enough to sustain a whole piece. That's very frustrating for me. Even after all of these years, I still think coming up with good ideas should be easy, but it's not. So I look for inspiration outside of my own head. I get ideas from the newspaper or the books I'm reading or stories someone has told me of moments in history, and then I try to come up with an idea that's all my own.

 **What's your best advice for teens who want to write historical fiction?**

Writing historical fiction takes time. Unlike your friends who may be writing contemporary stories, you'll be doing lots of research to make your story come alive and to assure its accuracy. But that's part of the fun of writing in this genre—finding those obscure details about your time period that fascinate, titillate, maybe even gross out your reader.

I like to rely on primary sources whenever I can. I interview people who've lived through the time period about which I'm writing, or I look at journals, diaries, or letters. I often read books that were written at that time so I get a sense of language and slang, and I watch movies or documentaries or go to plays set in that era so I can see how the actors move in their costumes. Since many of my stories are set during World War II, I look at catalogs or newspaper ads to tell me what people liked to buy.

Research is so much easier now that we have the Internet, but I never rely on facts I find online unless I can verify them on more than one reputable site or within my reference books.

And when you write dialogue, go easy on the historical slang. If you put in too much, your story will sound comical even if you don't intend it to. One or two period words per section are more than enough.

Historical fiction writers are lucky. We get to time travel, and we get to take our readers along for the ride!

NANCY GARDEN
http://www.nancygarden.com

Published books (complete list on website)
Annie on My Mind
Dove & Sword: A Novel of Joan of Arc
Good Moon Rising
Prisoner of Vampires
Peace, O River
Endgame
Nora and Liz

What do you find to be the easiest thing about writing?

The early stages of writing a book are the easiest for me—first, getting the original idea (I usually have several in my head all the time, stacked up and waiting to develop), and playing with it in my mind for a while until it seems ready to write. And writing the first draft often is also pretty easy. Everything seems possible at that early stage, and I can skip over things that need fixing because I know I can go back to them and fix them when I revise.

What do you find to be the hardest thing about writing?

Revising—which I do over and over and over again before I send a manuscript out to my agent or an editor. It's during that process that I deal with whatever problems the book has, and when I take parts of the book apart and try to put them together again or cut them. I usually let a manuscript sit for a long time

after the first or second draft—months, a year, or more—so I can see its flaws more clearly when I go back to it.

What's your best advice for teens who want to write fiction?

Read all you can, as often as you can. Read as widely as possible, but be sure to include the kinds of books and stories that you feel most drawn to and most inclined to write yourself. Read for pleasure and fun, yes, but also read to learn—notice words and sentences, dialogue and description; notice structure—the way the author tells the story, the way the plot strands fit together. Read books and articles about writing, too. And—of course—write! Keep a journal if that helps you—not a "what I did today" diary, but a record of your thoughts and ideas. Observe people and places and describe them in your journal. Write your thoughts about writing and about possible books; write your thoughts about what you've read and authors you admire.

Q&A

Author Q & A

ELISE LEONARD
http://www.eliseleonard.com

Published books
Al's World books:
   Monday Morning Blitz
   Killer Lunch Lady
   Scared Stiff
   Monkey Business
A LEEG of His Own books:
   Croaking Bullfrogs, Hidden Robbers
   20,000 LEEGs Under the C
   Failure to Lunch
   Hamlette
Junkyard Dan books
The Smith Brothers books
Leader books
Pete's Place books

(Note from Elise Leonard: I feel the need to tell you that I'm surrounded by guys. I'm married to one, have two sons, and every and all pets, animals, critters, rodents, insects, appliances, condiments, and more seem to be male in my household. So I can really relate to the male perspective and enjoy writing for guys.)

What do you find to be the easiest thing about writing?
The easiest thing is the commute! I roll out of bed, and there I am. I can even reach my big toe out from underneath the cov-

ers and turn on my computer and let it boot up while I'm still not quite ready to get out of bed. (Not many CEOs can say that, I'll bet!…And please note, I use the big toe of my right foot, not my left. I'm not toe-dexterous yet—but I keep trying. I figure that if I don't have the skill yet, I probably won't ever get it. But I keep hoping and trying.)

Other easy stuff: I get to go to work in my underwear. (And no, it's not a thong! If I had to wear a thong, it would be my answer for the next question.) I get to sit around and make up stories all day, every day. (For me, that's a pleasure—for other people, I'm told it would be a nightmare!)

What do you find to be the hardest thing about writing?

On the days I try to use the big toe on my left foot, I either get a horrible cramp or fall out of bed completely. (Not a good way to start your morning! Take my word.)

More hard stuff: It's hard to make a living. (The whole J. K. Rowling/Harry Potter thing is the exception—not the rule.) Rejections pretty much stink. People who write reviews without understanding my readership or my goals or my sense of humor are *really* hard to take! (Anyone know an available hit man? Only kidding!)

What's your best advice for teens who want to write fiction?

Buy, borrow, or steal a really comfortable chair. (You'll be sitting in it a lot!) Oh, and, everyone says, "Write what you know," but I like to say, "Write what you like." For me, I have a hard enough time trying to understand and deal with the real world much less other worlds, so for me, I like to write in contemporary time periods and use mostly realistic characters. (The closest I'll ever get to writing fantasy is when I write my name as "Mrs. Brad Pitt." The closest I'll ever get to writing sci-fi is when I write my sons a note to "Please, please clean your rooms" because it'll be a true tale of science fiction if it ever happens! Plus I'd probably have a heart attack if they ever did clean their rooms, or I'd die of some sort of plague from the gross fungus growing on the

bottom layer of whatever it is that's in their rooms, so I guess it's just as well!)

Remember that everyone likes something different—and that's *great!* I heard one book critic once say that she loves books that make her cry. For me, I've done my share of crying, so I don't want to read sad stories. I want to read books that make me laugh. But that's me. I'm not "emo" or "goth." I'm more like… "goof." And if, by chance, my style of writing pleases someone else, that's fantastic.

So at the risk of sounding like a mom (which I *am*) or a teacher (which I *was*), when you write, just be yourself. Be whatever is true to you—whether it's writing about werewolves, fairies, princes, vampires, historical figures, serial killers, school cliques, nobodies, whatever—write what interests *you!*

And I want to say one last thing. You have to write your story in the way that you feel your story comes across the best. No one but you can decide what that is. (But if someone you really, really respect gives you some advice that'll make your story better, and, if after thinking about it, you agree with that advice… take it. After all, the ultimate goal is to write a great story!)

DAVID LUBAR
http://www.davidlubar.com

Published books
True Talents
Hidden Talents
Sleeping Freshmen Never Lie
Dunk
Flip
Wizards of the Game
Invasion of the Road Weenies
The Curse of the Campfire Weenies
In the Land of the Lawn Weenies
Punished!
Dog Days
Accidental Zombie books:
    My Rotten Life
    Dead Guy Spy
    Goop Soup
    The Big Stink
    Enter the Zombie
Attack of the Vampire Weenies
The Battle of the Red Hot Pepper Weenies

What do you find to be the easiest thing about writing?

    I love writing dialogue. Once my characters start talking, everything just rolls. The only danger is that they'll end up standing around talking for too long when they should be out killing

vampires or riding dragons. It's easy to overdo the things you do well.

What do you find to be the hardest thing about writing?

I have a very hard time recapturing the pure joy of writing for its own sake. As soon as you start to achieve any amount of success or recognition, it's easy to imagine the world looking over your shoulder as you write. (Side note to the two or three of you who care about grammar—note the use of "its" and "it's" in the previous two sentences. If you keep this straight, you'll impress teachers, editors, and other important people.) I'm also bad at describing my characters. I hate to stop the action to narrate a mug shot of each person who appears.

What's your best advice for teens who want to write humorous fiction?

Expose yourself to all sorts of humor—stand-up comedy, cartoons (both the animated and the print varieties), jokes, song parodies, fiction, plays, light verse, etc. Don't be afraid to takes risks in your writing. Think of humor as a lot like horror—it involves events that are unexpected, surprising, and, fairly often, unpleasant. Be original. Be fresh. Try to look at things in different ways. Make connections nobody else notices. Most important of all—have fun. If you can make yourself laugh, you've created gold.

Q&A

CAROLYN MEYER
http://www.readcarolyn.com

Published books (complete list on website)
Young Royals series:
> *Mary, Bloody Mary*
> *Beware, Princess Elizabeth*
> *Doomed Queen Anne*
> *Patience, Princess Catherine*
> *Duchessina: A Novel of Catherine de' Medici*
> *The Bad Queen: Rules and Instructions for Marie*
> *Antoinette*

Royal Diary series:
> *Isabel, Jewel of Castilla*
> *Anastasia, Last Grand Duchess*
> *Kristina, The Girl King*

Where the Broken Heart Still Beats: The Story of Cynthia Ann Parker
Marie, Dancing
Loving Will Shakespeare
Cleopatra Confesses
The True Adventures of Charley Darwin
In Mozart's Shadow: His Sister's Story

What do you find to be the easiest thing about writing?

Getting new ideas. I'm often asked where I get ideas, and I can only say that they can come from just about anywhere. For instance, a visit to a museum with an exhibit of Degas sculptures, where I saw "Little Dancer Aged Fourteen" for the first

time, immediately sent my imagination spinning: What must it have been like to be the girl who posed for that sculpture? The result was *Marie, Dancing.* Another time, I picked up a pamphlet in a Dairy Queen in Texas that told the story of Quanah Parker—*Where the Broken Heart Still Beats* came out of that. A trip to a city park with a historical plaque suggested *White Lilacs.* Sometimes the ideas seem to come out of thin air. But they always come—the trick is to recognize the good ones.

What do you find to be the hardest thing about writing?

Accepting criticism. I always think whatever I've been laboring on for a year (that's how long the book usually takes me) and rewritten several times is perfect, a work of genius. My editor invariably thinks otherwise and sends back the manuscript with a 10-page list of "suggestions for improvement." Makes me want to scream! But I do it—sometimes I have to rewrite a novel three times until the editor is satisfied. She sets the bar very high! But my writing has certainly benefited, once I stopped pouting.

What's your best advice for teens who want to write historical fiction?

Read. Read, read, read! Keep a journal, to get in the habit of writing something every day. Learn the rules of grammar. Enjoy the research—that's the best part of it. Learn to accept criticism.

And read—did I mention that?

Q&A

TODD MITCHELL
http://www.toddmitchellbooks.com

Published books
The Traitor King
The Secret to Lying

What do you find to be the easiest thing about writing?

For me, the easiest thing about writing is coming up with ideas. The more stories I write, the more ideas I get. It's like breeding rabbits. (Did you know that in one year, a single pair of bunnies can give rise to more than a thousand offspring?)

What do you find to be the hardest thing about writing?

Letting go of things that aren't working is always hard for me. In order to know if a story will work out, I have to write my way into it. Sometimes, it's not until I'm fifty or a hundred pages along that I realize the story I set out to write isn't the story I should be writing. At that point, I usually try to let go of my original ideas, and I ask the characters what their story is. The quicker I can let go of things (the story I set out to write, the beginning that I thought was good, the dumb bunny metaphor that I loved) the quicker I'm able to move on and find something better. Nothing ever ends up the way I thought it would. That's what makes writing difficult, but it's also a good thing, because it keeps writing interesting. If I wasn't constantly discovering things by writing, I probably wouldn't do it.

Author Q & A

What's your best advice for teens who want to write fiction?

Write the book you most want to read. That's a loose paraphrase of something the writer John Gardner said. As simple as it sounds, thinking about that advice has helped me immensely to figure out what stories I want to tell and why. It's also kept me going through the hard times because it reminds me that there are stories that only I can tell, and if I don't write them, they won't exist. I think everyone has stories that only they can tell. But discovering what they are and making them real can be tricky.

Lauren Myracle

http://www.laurenmyracle.com

Published books

Bliss
Kissing Kate
Eleven
Twelve
Thirteen
TTYL
TTFN
L8R, G8R
Rhymes with Witches
The Fashion Disaster that Changed My Life
How to Be Bad (co-authored with E. Lockhart and
    Sarah Mlynowski)
Lov Ya Bunches
Violet in Bloom
Thirteen Plus One
BFF
Peace, Love, and Baby Ducks
Let It Snow (co-authored with John Green and Maureen John-
son)
Shine

What do you find to be the easiest thing about writing?

Nothing. Well, okay, I take that back. To write, you have to feed your brain with stories, right? Which means reading and reading and reading some more. I love that part!

What do you find to be the hardest thing about writing?

Everything. (Am I being annoying? Sorry!) Um, the hardest thing for me is…writing when I'd rather be watching "Grey's Anatomy." Writing when I'd rather be napping. Writing when I'd rather be e-mailing. All of those things are tempting—heck, everything is tempting when the alternative is sitting down and *working*. But like anything in life, you've got to be disciplined about what you love. So I remind myself, "Hey, this is your choice, whether you do it or not. So do it, you crazy fool!"

What's your best advice for teens who want to write fiction?

Read, read, read and write, write, write. Don't be afraid to write the crappy first draft, as Anne Lamott says (in slightly coarser language) in *Bird by Bird*. Remember that your first draft is "supposed" to suck. Your first draft is for you; it's how you figure out what your story is. *Then* you go back and make it better. Good luck, all you aspiring writers! You can do it!

DONITA K. PAUL
http://www.donitakpaul.com

Published books
The Dragon Keeper Chronicles:
  DragonSpell
  DragonQuest
  DragonKnight
  DragonFire
  DragonLight
Chiril Chronicles:
  Dragons of Chiril
  Dragons of the Valley
  Dragons of the Watch
Two Tickets to the Christmas Ball

What do you find to be the easiest thing about writing?

Ideas! Many times I have too many ideas to pursue. I'm fascinated by characters and want to explore their stories. I get caught by a fictional situation and want to know what characters are going to show up and how they will respond to the action and the challenges they face.

What do you find to be the hardest thing about writing?

Publishing! As a new writer it is so very, very hard to get in the door. After you've signed the contract, working with editors can be a joyful blessing or . . . not. Sometimes the cover artist has not caught the vision of the book and the cover looks like it belongs on someone else's novel. Sales numbers are lurking behind every conversation with your agent, publisher, marketing

department, and editor. I wish it were not true, but unless the sales numbers are good, your fantastic tale is doomed. But I will say that meeting the readers is the *best* part of being published. I do school visits and book signings and that is when I find delightful readers who are so enthusiastic and have so many great ideas.

What's your best advice for teens who want to write Christian novels?

By all means, do it! Don't try to preach a sermon, or get all the points of your preacher's last message into a tale, but rather weave in your chosen message subtly and without offense. Concentrate on the story, the characters, and the setting. I tell people I write about real people in real situations—people who have real problems and learn real lessons. Sometimes I get the response, "But you write fantasy!" Yes, but if my characters didn't ring true, if the reader could not relate to the characters' problems, if the reader couldn't accept the solutions as plausible, no one would read to the finish. After all, young and old people relate to the tomato and the cucumber [from *VeggieTales*] created by Phil Vischer and Mike Nawrocki. This is because they tackle relevant problems and solve them from a Christian, God-centered perspective. These two men are master storytellers. They get away with summarizing and verbalizing the "lesson," because of the format they use. But the successful Christian novelist takes a little different route. Rather than sticking to narrative format, he or she develops the story, paying attention to craft details such as dialogue, description, and reflection. The Christian worldview comes through because the author's heart is centered on Jesus and his or her tank is filled with God's Word.

I often say I am blessed to be doing something I love. I was a Sunday school teacher for decades. (We won't say how many.) In order to explain a concept, the teacher needs to understand it inside out. God has taught me so many wonderful lessons as I prepared to share His wisdom with others. And nothing is more rewarding than when a reader takes the time to write a note about some way God has touched his or her heart through the books I've written.

STEPHANIE PERKINS
http://www.stephanieperkins.com

Published books
Anna and the French Kiss
Lola and the Boy Next Door
Isla and the Happily Ever After (2012)

How did participating in NaNoWriMo (National Novel Writing Month) help you become a successful author?

I'm a terrible first-drafter—I'm slow, and I loathe the process—so the competitive spirit of NaNoWriMo has been a blessing for me, for ripping out that first ugly draft. The lightbulb went off when I realized that NaNo isn't about creating a good book, it's simply about creating a book. That took the pressure off. My final product (which has usually been through about 20 revisions) never looks much like its NaNo draft, but . . . without that crappy first draft, the final product would never happen, and I would never be published!

What do you find to be the easiest thing about writing?

Ideas. Ideas are everywhere! I love thinking up new projects or combining project ideas to create even better ones. I love the daydreaming, the planning, the research, the notes . . . all of that prep work. The problem is, of course, *none* of that is actually writing! C'est la vie.

What do you find to be the hardest thing about writing?

It's a toss-up between completing the first draft and seeing a project out through to its end. I've already discussed my problems with first drafts, but it can be equally challenging to finish the last few drafts. Most writers are incredibly sick of their own work by that point, and it's often impossible to see it with clear eyes. It makes revising and last-minute decision making very exhausting.

What's your best advice for teens who want to write romance into their fiction?

Make it real. Make it complicated. Make it magical.

LAURA RESAU
http://lauraresau.com

Published books
What the Moon Saw
Red Glass
The Queen of Water (co-authored with Maria Virginia Farinango)
The Ruby Notebook
The Indigo Notebook
Star in the Forest

What do you find to be the easiest thing about writing?

For me, the easiest thing is getting ideas for stories and books. Whenever I see glimpses of images or scenes or characters that could be part of a story, I jot down notes in my journal. My ideas come from everywhere—intriguing people and places I've encountered (around the world and in my own neighborhood), bits of dreams I've had, dusty old memories. Collecting story ideas feels like discovering a few scattered pieces of colored glass. I pick them up, examine them in the light, and then, little by little, page by page, I find more pieces, ultimately fitting them together into a kind of mosaic.

What do you find to be the hardest thing about writing?

The hardest thing for me is having the confidence to keep writing. Before *What the Moon Saw* was published, I was constantly doubting whether I was wasting my time by writing. After the book was well received, I worried that people might not

Author Q & A

like my second book, *Red Glass*. Now I have a contract for my future books, and I'm anxious that I won't be able to craft good manuscripts by my deadlines. I've come to accept that my insecurities are like a shape-shifting monster. I've learned that when the monster appears, the best I can do is just roll my eyes, give him a quick, annoyed sideways glance, and then keep writing.

What's your best advice for teens who want to write fiction?

Read lots of good books. Keep a journal and write whatever you want in it—poetry, stories, dreams, notes on books, odd things people say, character sketches, theories of existence, weird thoughts, surprising feelings. Don't worry whether your writing is good or not. Don't get frustrated if the vision in your head doesn't match what you put on paper. Don't expect perfection. Don't seek other people's approval, but do listen if they offer thoughtful, balanced feedback. Know that with every page you write—whether you think it's brilliant or horribly boring—you're becoming a better writer. Most of all, remember that writing can be pure magic if you let it.

OLUGBEMISOLA RHUDAY-PERKOVICH
http://www.olugbemisolabooks.com

Published books
8th Grade Superzero

What do you find to be the easiest thing about writing?

I am most comfortable creating characters, writing dialogue, and revising! I love to revise, to shape and reshape a story, get a little closer to the heart of what I hear and am trying to say. And I spend a lot of time thinking about my characters, putting them in different settings and situations, jotting down small details, habits, quirks, and characteristics that may or may not make it into the manuscript but help me get an idea of who they really are.

What do you find to be the hardest thing about writing?

That very first draft, that point somewhere in the middle where the doubts creep in, that critical voice starts speaking louder, where I wonder "Wait, what do I think I'm doing, trying to write a book?!" Getting past that point is very difficult for me, and I have to re-learn every time to drop the whole "perfectionist" thing, to keep moving forward even when I know it's not quite right, to be flexible, and to know that one bad day (or week, or month, or . . .) is not the end of the story.

Author Q & A

What's your best advice for teens who want to write multi-cultural novels?

Write full-bodied characters with full-bodied stories. We are none of us just the color of our skin, or our country of birth, or any one thing. We have many different stories to tell, all precious, both unique and universal. But maybe my best advice would be to write those stories! And don't give up!

LYNDA SANDOVAL
http://www.lyndasandoval.com

Published books
Who's Your Daddy?
Chicks Ahoy
"Party Foul," in *Breaking Up is Hard to Do*
The She Between Me and Marie
Father Knows Best

What do you find to be the easiest thing about writing?

Wow, is anything easy about writing? Ha! I guess my desire to tackle it is the easiest. It's a no-brainer. I wouldn't want to be doing anything else. The rest of it is hard and it doesn't get easier.

What do you find to be the hardest thing about writing?

PLOT! What the heck is plot? I'm a very intuitive writer, starting with a very rudimentary idea of what a given book will be about, and I write blind. I love it. It's like I discover the book as I'm writing it. And, hopefully, at the end, a plot is involved, but I don't ever write with one in mind.

What's your best advice for teens who want to write fiction?

Learn to trust your voice, your own way of seeing the world and expressing it on paper. Also (sorry, English teachers), once you get out of school, pass your SATs, etc., please, please forget everything they taught you about writing in school. It seems that high school English is heavily weighted toward the heinous passive tense "business" writing, which has no place in fiction. Learn all the rules of English and writing, all the literary devices, so that you'll understand when and why you're breaking them. But, mostly, TRUST YOUR VOICE.

Author Q & A

James Van Pelt

http://www.sff.net/people/james.van.pelt
Blog: jimvanpelt.livejournal.com

Published books
Strangers and Beggars
The Last of the O-Forms and Other Stories
Summer of the Apocalypse

What do you find to be the easiest thing about writing?

The easiest thing about writing is coming up with ideas to write about. I teach high school English, and a thousand dramas a day unfold around me. Every student is a story and has a story. All I have to do is pay attention. Of course, for a lot of people, coming up with an idea is the hard thing, which I think is because they don't realize that the idea isn't really all that important. The idea for the story doesn't have to be earth shattering. It just has to be interesting to the writer. What makes the idea good in the story is what the writer does with it.

When I assign short stories to my students, it is inevitable that a few of them will come up with an idea and tell me about it. Sometimes they can spend a *long* time telling me the idea. When they're done, I always tell them the same thing, no matter how interesting or how lame the idea sounds: "Sounds good. Go ahead and try it." I can say that because it is true. The idea doesn't make the story good. Only how the idea is handled makes it good.

What do you find to be the hardest thing about writing?

I've been writing for what seems like a long time now, and I enjoy all of the process, from deciding what I want to write about, to typing my name and address in the upper left corner of the first blank page, to actually composing the piece (including those long moments where I'm just staring at my computer screen while thinking about what to do next), to realizing I know the end of the story and can push toward it, to revising. None of them are hard.

What is hard is realizing that I don't have time to do all I want. Teaching school, being a father, owning a house, mowing the lawn, sleeping, etc., all take time away from the writing. My time is committed to other things, and writing is slow. When I'm really rolling—I mean *really* rolling—I can compose about 1,000 words in an hour. Five hundred words is more typical in an hour, though, and it's not unusual to be at my computer that long and do less. If I had four or five hours a day to devote to writing, I could be more productive, but I don't. An hour or two is it most days. What is hard are the interruptions.

J. R. R. Tolkien wrote a wonderful short story called "A Leaf by Niggle." In it, an amateur painter named Niggle wanted more than anything in the world to work on a huge painting of a tree, but life kept interfering. His relatives would come to visit, or a neighbor would need help mending his roof. Niggle couldn't work, and because of that his painting of a tree was never as good as he could make it. The tree never came together. Every once in a while he would do a pretty good leaf, though, and he took some consolation in that. I feel a little that way now and then. My vision of what I'd like to do is never quite as good as I would like to make it, but every once in a while I compose a sentence that really pleases me. If only I had more time.

What's your best advice for teens who want to write horror?

In some ways, horror is easy. If you are writing a story that says, basically, "Something awful out there is going to get you," then you are writing horror. The blood and gore and images of death that people sometimes associate with horror are just the

trappings of a horror story, not the heart. The heart of horror is in that feeling that we are helpless. The bad thing is on the way. It makes me shiver right now to think of it.

So, my best advice to a teen who wants to write horror is to not let the props that often stand on the horror stage distract you. Horror is not about zombies or vampires or serial killers. It's about realizing that you can't get away.

Now, knowing that there is no escape, let your characters try as hard as they can to not lose. The struggle is what makes horror interesting. Struggle is what makes all stories interesting. If your character manages to beat whatever was pursuing him at the end, whether it is something slithery that lives under the bed, or a shadow that lurks only in the peripheral vision, or the footsteps behind him as he walks through an empty hall, then he delayed the inevitable because he struggled and got lucky. Next time, or the time after that, or some time in the far future, he won't.

Think about what scares you. I have a lot of fears: nuclear war, animal attacks, tornados, disease. You probably have a list, too. Now, think about how you feel when you are faced with your fears. Write a story that makes your reader feel that. Horror isn't about telling the reader what happened; it's about making the reader feel something about it while it's happening.

Q&A

DENISE VEGA
http://www.denisevega.com

Published books
Click Here (To Find Out How I Survived Seventh Grade)
Access Denied (And Other Eighth-Grade Messages)
Fact of Life #31
Rock On (2012)

What do you find to be the easiest thing about writing?

The easiest thing is coming up with the ideas. I have tons of ideas—all of them brilliant, of course—and I can't wait to make each and every one of them into a brilliant book. I love the excitement of a new idea, the way it grabs me and won't let go, teasing me like a big piece of chocolate held just outside my reach. This is the time when I can dream the story, imagine the possibilities, convinced it will be as well-written and engaging as my favorite books of the same genre, with readers clamoring for it in droves. Idea-time is where I allow fantasy to enter my reality because if you aren't excited about an idea, how can you expect readers to be?

What do you find to be the hardest thing about writing?

The hardest thing is finishing the first draft of that brilliant idea and realizing that I may not have the skill or talent to make it as brilliant as the fantasy image I had during the idea stage. I tend to start writing before I even have an inkling of where I might be going so I often find myself stalled partway into it.

However, I learn new things with each book. I'm not an outliner and never will be, but I have begun to *prewrite*, which seems to help me become less blocked during the actual writing. This is where I jot down bits of dialogue between characters, parts of scenes, plot points and such, so the book simmers in the back of my mind until I'm ready to work on it. Also, since my books tend to be character-driven, I try to define the emotional growth arc my main character will go through—for example, in my book *Fact of Life #31*, I knew that my main character Kat would move from being intimidated by and feeling inadequate around her mother to recognizing her own unique strengths and qualities and being proud of them. Once I'm able to define that character arc, I have a bit of a light in the darkness and can feel my way a little more easily to the end of the first draft.

The other hard thing for me is trying not to revise as I go because it tends to slow down the process and often makes me lose the thread of my story. Sometimes it's okay, but now I'm trying to just flip back and jot a note to myself about what I'm thinking of changing or adding, and then forging ahead. Revision is my favorite part of writing so I tend to do it while writing the first draft instead of just getting things down so I can begin the actual revising!

What's your best advice for teens who want to write fiction?

Read, read, read, write, write, write, and revise, revise, revise. I think it's important to read all kinds of fiction, especially the type that you like to write. Some people think this can taint your own storytelling, but for me it provides an opportunity to be in a world like the one I'm trying to create. I can absorb the writing style and character development of a gifted writer, and it helps get me in the mood and tone of my own story.

And I would encourage any writer to focus on the writing first and worry about publication later. The competition is too fierce not to present your very best work to a publisher—spend the time you need to improve your craft. My first published novel, *Click Here (To Find Out How I Survived Seventh Grade)*, was the sixth novel for young people I'd actually written. The *sixth*.

I have five other books hanging out in my closet, all practice. I don't consider any of them a waste because what I learned from those got me to my first published book.

Second piece of advice: Get feedback on your work from someone you trust and who has good judgment about writing and books. If at all possible, let that be another writer or writers with some experience. And listen to the advice, trying things out. The work is ultimately yours, but other people can give you insight into where things are dragging, where a character or situation isn't believable, what you might try to heighten the conflict.

When you're first getting feedback, you may try everything because you aren't sure what will work. Later, you will become more in tune with what may or may not jive with the vision of your story and be able to sift through the feedback in a different way. But I listen to all the feedback I get and have been amazed at the direction my books have taken after I've considered feedback I've received.

QUESTIONS AND ANSWERS

CHAPTER FOURTEEN

QUESTIONS AND ANSWERS

**Sometimes questions are more
important than answers.**
—Nancy Willard

I've led many writing workshops with teens. Naturally, questions come up. In this chapter, I've tried to include the questions that are most often asked.

How long does it take to write a book?

As long as it does.

I know that sounds flippant, but it's perfectly true. Tolkien worked on *The Lord of the Rings* for twenty-five years. Some practiced novelists can write a whole novel in a couple of months. It took me over five years to write my first book, three years to write my second, and two to write my third. Thank goodness it only takes a few hours to read a book that requires years to write! If it didn't work that way, there would be very few jobs open for novelists.

It will take you as long as it takes you. The more you write, the more you'll find your own pace.

Where do you write?

It depends on what part of the process I'm in. If it's the dreaded first draft, I look for a place where I can tune out my critical mind—the one that's telling me this story is hopeless—and tune in to my creative mind. So I might write under a tree, sitting on a rock next to a trail, or leaning against a pillow in a corner of my house. Every once in a while I get together with a writing buddy, and we both sit in a coffee shop and see how much we can get done. We're not working on the same thing, but just being in the company of someone else who is also wrestling with a story can be helpful.

The next phase happens at the computer. I have a desktop, so I go into my office. Sometimes I pick out theme music to help me stay in the right mood for a particular scene.

After a draft is printed, I carry it somewhere else and go over it with a pen, marking it up. Some pages get tossed. Others get revised, again and again.

Do you write at the same time every day, or do you wait for inspiration?

I don't wait for inspiration. Well, let me clarify. To me, there are different kinds of inspiration. There's the overall inspiration that comes from the idea of the story itself—the characters at work in your heart, the plot twisting and turning in your mind, the setting showing itself to your inner vision. I do rely upon that kind of inspiration, heavily. But then there are those bursts of intense creative activity that are sometimes called inspiration. I don't wait for those bursts. If I did, I'd write about two chapters a year.

When I'm focused on finishing a book, I give myself daily deadlines for chapters or scenes. I might write them in the morning or the evening, but I'm going to write them. Other writers approach things in their own way. Some have strict writing hours or page requirements ("Eight hours a day," or "Three chapters a week" or "A book every six months"). There's no formula, except that serious writers find some way to keep going.

Do you use any specific rituals to help you write?

Yes.

Authors have many ways to get themselves to write. I heard one writer say she wears the same sweatshirt every day while writing until she finishes the book she's working on. The catch? She "can't" wash the sweatshirt until she's done with the book. That's her way of motivating herself.

I like to move around a lot; I stand up and walk around every ten minutes or so, do weird "brain exercises" that are hard to explain, or dash madly down the street and then crane my neck to stare at the clouds.

Tea also helps.

Authors have many ways to get themselves to write.

Did anyone encourage you to write when you were younger?

I attended fifth grade in Lexington, MA. My teacher was a tall man with a booming voice. He liked to read aloud. He would pound on his desk with his fist as he read "The Telltale Heart," by Edgar Allen Poe. He assigned us book reports, essays, and stories.

At the end of the year he sought me out. "I hear you're moving away," he said.

"Yes. To Wisconsin. My dad got transferred."

"I just have one thing to say to you. Never let anything keep you from writing," he said, and walked off.

I didn't know at the time that his words would dig down into my heart and live there like dormant seeds for years and years. I wish I could thank him now, but he has passed away.

When I was younger, I didn't show my writing much. Too shy, back then. Later, I got great support from my children, my sisters, and my husband Tim. And friends along the way have been wonderfully encouraging as well.

But although encouragement is delightful, it's a small part of the reason I write. Mostly I just feel as if I *must* write, must create stories, must explore my imagination. Writing is part of me, just like love of family and friends. It's not something I feel like I could choose to stop.

Did anyone discourage you from writing?

The main discouragement has come from people saying "You can't make a living writing."

Now I make my living writing and speaking, and I haven't had a "regular" job for years. This is delightful, but it's also not the reason I write. If all the books in the world suddenly ceased to be, I would still write.

How important are titles?

Titles are meant to intrigue readers and give a glimpse of what a story is about. Coming up with a good title can be challenging, and excellent writers sometimes get it wrong—for example, the original title for Robert Louis Stevenson's *Treasure Island* was *The Sea Cook*. Jane Austen initially wrote *Pride and Prejudice* under the title *First Impressions*.

When you come up with a title, run it by a few people who haven't read your story. Watch their faces. Do they light up or power down? Do they say "Ooh," or do they say "Uh-huh" without enthusiasm?

Some say a book's title and the art on the cover are more important than the book itself—when it comes to sales. That's a little disconcerting to an author, but it seems to be true. Authors don't design their own covers by the way. And sometimes, for marketing reasons, publishers ask authors to change their titles.

My English teacher is always talking about symbols in literature. What's so important about symbols?

Symbols can be a wonderful way to say something without coming out and saying it.

For example, in Laura Resau's novel *Red Glass*, images of red glass appear in several places. Each time, the vivid glass represents the triumph of life over death, love over hate, courage over fear. During various hardships and tragedies, the red glass keeps showing itself in various shapes and sizes—shards, bottles, mosaics, and beads. The unstated message tells us that life, love, and courage are available no matter what. Resau could have chosen to use the voice of Sophie, her protagonist, to say something like, "We can all experience life, love, and courage even in the face of disaster." But by using symbolism instead, her message is richer and deeper.

If you find yourself trying to force a symbol into your story, it probably isn't going to work. But symbols may naturally occur to you as you write, and when they do, they'll give an extra layer to your writing.

What courses should I take in college if I want to be a writer? Should I get a degree in creative writing?

There's not necessarily any correlation between success as a writer and professional training. Personally, I had no educational writing qualifications when I got published—which is true for many authors. However, some people have found that studying writing in college helped them become better writers.

If you're headed to college and want to be a writer, my recommendation is to take all the writing classes you want but get your degree in a different field entirely—preferably one with practical applications. That way you won't have to live under the strain of trying to make a living as a writer when you graduate college. (Even a master's degree in creative writing is no guarantee of employment anywhere, nor is it a guarantee of getting published.) Pick a field you're interested in, of course. Then you can make a living as you build up your writing career, and you're less likely to fall prey to fear and self-doubt. Your writing won't be tied to your survival.

Symbols can be a wonderful way to say something without coming out and saying it.

180

How much grammar should I study if I want to be an author?

Grammar. That's a subject authors do not necessarily love or even like, a subject many find confusing and overwhelming. And yet, grammar is always used when telling stories—because grammar lurks within language, whether that language is spoken or written.

Lots of writers do not consciously understand grammar. I have no idea how to analyze sentences in terms of participles or gerunds. If I had to take a test on grammatical terms, I'd flunk.

But that's not the part of grammar that writers need to know. We need to put words together into sentences and sentences into paragraphs—in ways that work for storytelling. To do this, we rely on a feeling for the music of words and how they fit together. Grammar is a part of that process, but it doesn't have to be visible on the surface. We don't have to be experts on grammatical theory to write well.

The easiest way to unconsciously study written grammar is by reading. Read, read, read, and read some more. You'll get a feeling for the structure and rhythm of the written word. You'll take it into your pores, and it will find its way to your bones.

I often begin a story, get bored and start a new one. How do you manage to stay with one story until it's finished?

It's natural to do a lot of starting and stopping when you're first getting into writing, and I did that too, many times. It's a way of testing your wings as a writer. When you get bored with a story, there's nothing wrong with dropping it or moving on to your next idea. Sometimes a story needs to be left alone for awhile, and then when you come back to it you have fresh energy for it.

Just don't let too much time go by without writing at all. You can freewrite every day without having to stick to any particular topic or idea.

I want a career as a writer. How do I get published?

This simple question doesn't have a simple answer. In fact, the subject is so complicated that in my book *Wild Ink*—a writing guide geared to adults—there are two chapters devoted to submitting manuscripts and getting published.

If you've written a novel, the main way of getting published is through a traditional publisher, which is how the authors you've found in bookstores and on library shelves have been published. This involves sending your manuscript directly to editors at publishing companies, or to agents you hope will agree to

Grammar lurks within language, whether that language is spoken or written.

represent you to publishing companies. If an agent likes your work enough to represent you, he or she will do the work of trying to find a publisher.

Writer's Market is a resource helpful to career-minded writers. It's a fat book available in nearly any bookstore or library. It lists publishers, addresses, what each company says it is looking for, and other important details and tips about approaching publishers and agents.

If you've written a short story that could be published in a magazine, you'll need to research which magazines publish fiction and study their submission guidelines. You'll find information about magazines in *Writer's Market,* too.

Writing contests sometimes reward winners with publication. (Carefully research each of them before sending any entry fees. Find out if the contest is legitimate and has a good reputation.) *Writer's Market* also lists writing contests.

Be aware that traditional publishers will never ask you to share the costs of publishing your book. So watch out if a "publisher" tells you there are charges involved.

Self-publishing is another option more writers are taking, and writers who self-publish must pay a printer. Before going this route—or any other that involves costs to you—do some in-depth investigating to be sure you've found the best option.

What's the most important thing I need to know before trying to get published?

Besides having a great story? I recommend learning an important skill: how to deal with rejection. Ah, rejection. It's only a three-syllable word, but it's also a very big topic that virtually all authors learn about, whether we want to or not.

Competition in the publishing world is fierce. Depending upon the type of book you're writing, it can be just as intense as the competition to play for a professional sports team. Thousands of rejection letters are sent out to aspiring writers every month by agents and publishing companies.

We all deal with rejection in our own way. Some of us try to find humor in our rejections. Some of us cry and feel wounded. Some instantly start a new project as a way to forget about the one that was rejected. Some keep trying over and over, revising and resubmitting the same story—which sometimes works. As with everything else about writing, there isn't one method that works for all.

If you get torn up when someone rejects or criticizes something you've written, if you feel paralyzed or seriously depressed about it, please wait to send out your manuscript until you can separate your writing from your self-esteem. If all

Writer's Market *is a resource helpful to career-minded writers.*

your confidence is tied to your story, you'll be at the mercy of cold-sounding rejection letters. It won't hurt anything to wait, and it may help.

What do you wish you could do differently if you were starting over with writing?

Quite honestly, I wish I could have read a book like this. Much of the information in *Seize the Story* took me years to figure out or understand.

The other thing I wish I could change has to do with confidence. The only reason I was able to finish my first book, *The Seer and the Sword*, was because I told myself it didn't matter if anyone but my children and I ever read it. I stalled myself repeatedly by listening to my critical mind say the story wasn't any good.

If you could become an author all over again, what would you do the same?

I would stay with the stories that haunt me most. I'd remember that in the realm of storytelling, creative intuition is far more powerful than logic. I'd read everything I could get my hands on. While writing, I'd set aside the world and just focus on what's happening in my imagination. I'd keep communicating with my characters and be grateful. Most of all, I would honor the writer within.

May I send you a story I've written and get your feedback?

No. The only time I critique stories is during live workshops. If I said "yes" to one person I would feel obligated to say "yes" to everyone. I still want to write my own stories, and I'd have no time for that if I were to read and critique all the stories people want to send me.

What is the most enjoyable thing about being an author?

The freedom to create stories is a feeling like no other. When I wake up in the morning thinking about a scene in a chapter, I smile to myself. And when something in my life is dark or sad, I know I can take that darkness or sadness and transform it into a good story.

It's also rewarding to hear from readers who love what I've written, readers who enter the worlds of my novels and share my imagination.

If you could give me just one piece of advice about writing fiction, what would it be?

I'll cheat on this question and give two pieces of advice: read and write. The more you read, the more you absorb an understanding of writing. The more you

Thousands of rejections are sent out to aspiring writers every month by publishing companies.

write, the more you develop a strong relationship with the writer you have inside. Getting to know that inner writer is like making a friend who will never be lost, a friend who will help you open your creative imagination, a friend who will still be with you after your stories are ready for the world to read. Invaluable.

The freedom to create stories is a feeling like no other.

ACKNOWLEDGMENTS

Many thanks to editor Cheri Thurston, who believed in this book despite a sketchy proposal and terrible first draft. Zach Howard drew the wonderful illustration on the cover. Thanks also to the new publisher, Prufrock Press, and its staff for developing this new edition.

My son, Emrys, took time out from his performing schedule to read a draft of *Seize the Story* and make helpful and entertaining comments. My husband, Tim, encouraged me from start to finish. My daughter, Rose, gave a thousand smiles while in the midst of a heavy school schedule. And my sisters, Peggy and Bridget, cheered from afar.

Rebecca Rowley, writing buddy extraordinaire, put up with me switching to nonfiction in midstream of a novel.

Big gratitude to all the busy authors who made time for interviews. Special thanks to those who contributed story excerpts and gave permission to print them: David Lubar, Todd Mitchell, Laura Resau, Teresa R. Funke, Denise Vega, James Van Pelt, and Elise Leonard.

And perhaps most of all, thanks to all the teens who have joined my writing workshops and taught me what they most wanted to know about how to seize a story.

BIBLIOGRAPHY

Adams, Richard. *Watership Down*. New York: Scribner, 2005.

Andersen, Hans Christian. *Hans Christian Andersen: The Complete Fairy Tales and Stories*. New York: Anchor Books, 1983.

Austen, Jane. *Pride and Prejudice*. New York: Book-of-the-Month Club, 1996.

Barrie, J. M. *Peter Pan: The Original Story*. New York: Harper Festival, 2003.

Baum, L. Frank. *The Wonderful Wizard of Oz*. Boston: Adamant Media Corporation, 2000.

Bauer, Joan. *Hope Was Here*. New York: Puffin, 2005.

Beowulf. Trans. Burton Raffel. New York: Signet Classics, 1999.

Bickham, Jack M. *Setting*. Cincinnati, Ohio: Writer's Digest Books, 1999.

Booker, Christopher. *The Seven Basic Plots*. London: Continuum, 2004.

Brewer, Robert. *2008 Writer's Market*. Cincinnati, Ohio: Writer's Digest Books, 2008.

Brontë, Charlotte. *Jane Eyre*. Hertfordshire, England: Wordsworth Classics, 1994.

Butler, Robert Olen. *From Where You Dream*. New York: Grove Press, 2005.

Carroll, Lewis. *Alice's Adventures In Wonderland*. New York: Dial, 2006.

Collodi, Carlo. *Pinocchio*. New York: Penguin Classics, 2002.

Collins, Suzanne. *The Hunger Games*. New York: Scholastic Press, 2008.

Conrad, Barnaby, and the staff of the Santa Barbara Writers' Conference. *The Complete Guide to Writing Fiction*. Cincinnati, Ohio: Writer's Digest Books, 1990.

Coville, Bruce. *Jeremy Thatcher, Dragon Hatcher.* Orlando, Florida: Harcourt, 2002.

Dickens, Charles. *A Christmas Carol.* New York: Puffin Classics, 2001.

Dumas, Alexandre. *The Three Musketeers.* Hertfordshire, England: Wordsworth Classics, 1997.

Elliott, L. M. *Under A War-Torn Sky.* New York: Hyperion, 2003.

Farmer, Nancy. *The Sea of Trolls.* New York: Simon Pulse, 2006.

Funke, Cornelia. *Inkheart.* New York: Scholastic Press, 2005.

Funke, Teresa R. *Remember Wake.* Fort Collins, Colorado: Bailiwick Press, 2007.

Grimm, Brothers. *Tales of the Brothers Grimm.* New York: Book-of-the-Month Club, 1999.

Hanley, Victoria. *The Seer and the Sword.* New York: Laurel Leaf, 2003.

---. *The Healer's Keep.* New York: Laurel Leaf, 2005.

---. *The Light of the Oracle.* New York: Laurel Leaf, 2006.

Homer. *The Odyssey.* New York: Penguin Classics, 2003.

Lee, Harper. *To Kill A Mockingbird.* New York: Harper Classics, 2006.

LeGuin, Ursula K. *A Wizard of Earthsea.* New York: Spectra, 2004.

Leland, Christopher T. *The Creative Writer's Style Guide.* Cincinnati, Ohio: Writer's Digest Books, 2002.

Leonard, Elise. Scene contributed by the author.

Levin, Donna. *Get That Novel Written!* Cincinnati, Ohio: Writer's Digest Books, 2001.

Lubar, David. Scenes contributed by the author.

Maass, Donald. *Writing the Breakout Novel.* Cincinnati, Ohio: Writer's Digest Books, 2002.

Marshall, Evan. *The Marshall Plan for Novel Writing.* Cincinnati, Ohio: Writer's Digest Books, 2001.

Meyer, Stephenie. *Twilight.* New York: Little, Brown Young Readers, 2006.

Mitchell, Todd. *The Traitor King.* New York: Scholastic Press, 2007.

Montgomery, R.A. *Choose Your Own Adventure Series.* Waitsfield, Vermont: Chooseco, 2006.

Myracle, Lauren. *Thirteen.* New York: Dutton, 2008.

Resau, Laura. *What the Moon Saw.* New York: Yearling, 2008.

---. *Red Glass.* New York: Delacorte Press, 2007.

Rowling, J.K. *Harry Potter and the Sorcerer's Stone.* New York: Scholastic Press, 2006.

---. *Harry Potter and the Goblet of Fire.* New York: Scholastic Press, 2006.

Shakespeare, William. *The Complete Works of William Shakespeare*. New York, Chatham River Press, 1987.

Stoker, Bram. *Dracula*. New York: Penguin Classics, 2003.

Strunk, William, and White, E.B. *The Elements of Style*. Boston: Allyn & Bacon, 2000.

Szeman, Sherri. *Mastering Point of View*. Cincinnati, Ohio: Story Press, 2001.

Tolkien, J. R. R. *The Lord of the Rings*. New York: Houghton-Mifflin, 2005.

Van Pelt, James. *The Radio Magician and Other Stories*. Bonney Lake, Michigan: Fairwood Press, 2009.

Vega, Denise. Scene contributed by the author.

Wilbers, Stephen. *Keys to Great Writing*. Cincinnati, Ohio: Writer's Digest Books, 2007

ABOUT THE AUTHOR

Victoria Hanley spent years preparing for a writing career by holding as many contrasting jobs as possible, from baking bread to teaching anatomy and hosting radio shows. She's traveled throughout the continental U.S. by car, plane, bus, train, and bicycle. She blames the influence of restless pioneer ancestors for the fact that she's lived in forty places in six states from the West to the East Coast.

After gathering a large database of character traits by closely observing various people during the course of her travels and jobs, she decided to use her imagination to write fantasy. To her surprise, her books won awards and honors both at home and abroad. She now lives in Loveland, CO, near the foothills of the Rockies.

You can visit her website at http://www.victoriahanley.com

INDEX

Adams, Richard, 87

Alice's Adventures in Wonderland, 87

Andersen, Hans Christian, 86

antagonist, 11, 16–18, 21, 25, 27, 29, 57, 75, 82, 94

Aristotle, 34

Austen, Jane, 11, 87, 179

Barrie, J. M., 87

Barron, T. A., 134–135

Bauer, Joan, 34, 136–138

Baum, L. Frank, 87

Bell, Hilari, 34, 139–141

Beowulf, 34

Booker, Christopher, 86–89, 99

Brontë, Charlotte, 11

cadence, 111–112

Calhoun, Dia, 142

career in writing, 176–183

Carroll, Lewis, 87

characterization, 28–30
    falling out of character, 28–29
    flaws, 29
    stereotypes, 29–30

characters, 9–30
    appearance, 11–12
    contrasting, 16–17
    goals, 20
    introducing, 13–14
    motivation, 18–19
    naming, 14–15
    perspective, 21–24
    primary, 25–26
    secondary, 25–27
    stakes, 18–20
    traits, 27–28

Choose Your Own Adventure, 120

Christmas Carol, A, 87

"Cinderella," 26, 66, 85–86, 100

Clancy, Tom, 100

climax, 99–100

college courses, 180

Collins, Suzanne, 93

complications, 97–99

conflicts, 93–96
    external, 94–95
    internal, 95–96

Coville, Bruce, 121

creative writing degree, 180

criticism, 3, 60, 105–107, 155

critiques, 105–107
    classroom, 106
    helpful, 105–106
    unhelpful, 106

Crutcher, Chris, 143–144

de-cluttering, 108–110

denouement, 100

dialogue, 63–75
    brackets, 67
    common problems with, 70–74
    formatting, 74–75
    subtext, 69
    tags, 67–68

Dickens, Charles, 87

discouragement, 179

Dracula, 86

Dumas, Alexandre, 86

Elliott, L. M., 35

encouragement, 179

ending, 100–101

FAQ's, 177–184

Farmer, Nancy, 121

first drafts, 4–6, 113, 140, 147, 159

first person point of view, 117–119
    advantages, 118
    disadvantages, 119

Fowler, Gene, 4

freewriting, 3–6, 47, 60

"Frog Prince, The," 88

Funke, Cornelia, 123

Funke, Teresa R., 71 145–146

Garden, Nancy, 147–148

grammar, 3, 140, 148, 153, 155, 181

Grimm, Brothers, 26, 86, 88

Harry Potter and the Goblet of Fire, 21
Harry Potter and the Sorcerer's Stone, 11, 93
Healer's Keep, The, 5, 21, 34, 45
Homer, 87
Hope Was Here, 34
Hunger Games, The, 11, 93–94

in media res, 34, 99, 129
Inkheart, 123
inspiration, 106, 145, 178

Jane Eyre, 11
Jeremy Thatcher, Dragon Hatcher, 121
Julius Caesar, 87

Lee, Harper, 118
LeGuin, Ursula K., 123
Leonard, Elise, 96–97, 149–151
Light of the Oracle, The, 35
Lord of the Rings, The, 87, 99–100, 123, 177
Lubar, David, 13–14, 54–55, 152–153

Meyer, Carolyn, 154–155
Meyer, Stephenie, 93, 118
Mitchell, Todd, 26–27, 44, 66, 156–157
Montgomery, R. A., 120
Much Ado About Nothing, 87
Myracle, Lauren, 118, 158–159

Odyssey, The, 87
outlining, 33–34
overwriting, 112–113

passive voice, 110–111
Paul, Donita K., 160–161
Perkins, Stephanie, 162–163
Peter Pan, 85, 87
plot, 85–89
Poe, Edgar Allen, 179
point of view, 117–126
    first person, 117–119
    choosing, 125–126
    second person, 120
    third person, 121–125
POV. See point of view

Pride and Prejudice, 11, 87, 179
protagonist, 11, 16–20, 25–29, 35–36, 44, 57, 75, 82, 87, 94–95, 99, 123
publishing, 160, 180–182

Red Glass, 44, 164–165, 180
rejection, 178–179
Remember Wake, 71
Resau, Laura, 43–44, 46–47, 49, 164–165, 180
rituals, 178
Rhuday-Perkovich, Olugbemisola, 166–167
Romeo and Juliet, 87
Rowling, J. K., 11, 21, 93, 150

Sandoval, Lynda, 168
scenes, 29, 33–36
Sea of Trolls, 121
second person point of view, 117, 120, 126
    advantages, 120
    disadvantages, 120
Seer and the Sword, The, 34, 85, 99, 183
self-publishing, 182
setting, 39–49, 82
    common problems, 46–48
Seven Basic Plots, The, 86–88, 99
Shakespeare, 87
showing, 66, 79–82
"Sleeping Beauty," 87
Stevenson, Robert Louis, 179
Stoker, Bram, 86
style and word choice, 53, 107
style and voice, 53–55
suspension of disbelief, 41
symbols, 180
telling, 79–82
"Telltale Heart, The," 179
third person point of view, 121–125
    limited, 121–123
        advantages, 123
        disadvantages, 123
    omniscient, 123–125
        advantages, 125
        disadvantages, 125
Thirteen, 118
"Three Little Pigs, The," 35
Three Musketeers, The, 86

titles, 179–180
To Kill a Mockingbird, 118
Tolkien, J. R. R., 87, 99, 123, 166
Traitor King, The, 44
Treasure Island, 179
trimming, 72–73, 112–113
Twain, Mark, 79, 107
Twilight, 93, 118

"Ugly Duckling, The," 86
Under a War-Torn Sky, 35

Van Pelt, James, 55, 111, 169–171
Vega, Denise, 54, 172–174
voice, 53–55, 60, 126, 134, 168
Vonnegut, Kurt, 34, 93

Watership Down, 87
What the Moon Saw, 44, 164
Wild Ink, 181
Wizard of Earthsea, A, 123
Wonderful Wizard of Oz, The, 85, 87
word choice, 53, 107–108
writer's block, 58–60
Writer's Market, 182
writing contests, 182

COMMON CORE STATE
STANDARDS ALIGNMENT

Grade Level	Common Core State Standards
Grade 7 ELA-Literacy	RL.7.6 Analyze how an author develops and contrasts the points of view of different characters or narrators in a text.
	W.7.3 Write narratives to develop real or imagined experiences or events using effective technique, relevant descriptive details, and well-structured event sequences.
	W.7.5 With some guidance and support from peers and adults, develop and strengthen writing as needed by planning, revising, editing, rewriting, or trying a new approach, focusing on how well purpose and audience have been addressed. (Editing for conventions should demonstrate command of Language standards 1–3 up to and including grade 7 here.)
	W.7.10 Write routinely over extended time frames (time for research, reflection, and revision) and shorter time frames (a single sitting or a day or two) for a range of discipline-specific tasks, purposes, and audiences.
	L.7.3 Use knowledge of language and its conventions when writing, speaking, reading, or listening.
	L.7.5 Demonstrate understanding of figurative language, word relationships, and nuances in word meanings.
Grade 8 ELA-Literacy	RL.8.3 Analyze how particular lines of dialogue or incidents in a story or drama propel the action, reveal aspects of a character, or provoke a decision.
	RL.8.6 Analyze how differences in the points of view of the characters and the audience or reader (e.g., created through the use of dramatic irony) create such effects as suspense or humor.
	W.8.3 Write narratives to develop real or imagined experiences or events using effective technique, relevant descriptive details, and well-structured event sequences.
	W.8.5 With some guidance and support from peers and adults, develop and strengthen writing as needed by planning, revising, editing, rewriting, or trying a new approach, focusing on how well purpose and audience have been addressed. (Editing for conventions should demonstrate command of Language standards 1–3 up to and including grade 8 here.)
	W.8.10 Write routinely over extended time frames (time for research, reflection, and revision) and shorter time frames (a single sitting or a day or two) for a range of discipline-specific tasks, purposes, and audiences.
	L.8.1 Demonstrate command of the conventions of standard English grammar and usage when writing or speaking.
	L.8.3 Use knowledge of language and its conventions when writing, speaking, reading, or listening.
	L.8.5 Demonstrate understanding of figurative language, word relationships, and nuances in word meanings.

Grade Level	Common Core State Standards
Grade 9-10 ELA-Literacy	RL.9-10.5 Analyze how an author's choices concerning how to structure a text, order events within it (e.g., parallel plots), and manipulate time (e.g., pacing, flashbacks) create such effects as mystery, tension, or surprise.
	W.9-10.3 Write narratives to develop real or imagined experiences or events using effective technique, well-chosen details, and well-structured event sequences.
	W.9-10.5 Develop and strengthen writing as needed by planning, revising, editing, rewriting, or trying a new approach, focusing on addressing what is most significant for a specific purpose and audience. (Editing for conventions should demonstrate command of Language standards 1–3 up to and including grades 9–10 here.)
	W.9-10.10 Write routinely over extended time frames (time for research, reflection, and revision) and shorter time frames (a single sitting or a day or two) for a range of tasks, purposes, and audiences.
	L.9-10.1 Demonstrate command of the conventions of standard English grammar and usage when writing or speaking.
	L.9-10.5 Demonstrate understanding of figurative language, word relationships, and nuances in word meanings.
Grade 11-12 ELA-Literacy	RL.11-12.3 Analyze the impact of the author's choices regarding how to develop and relate elements of a story or drama (e.g., where a story is set, how the action is ordered, how the characters are introduced and developed).
	RL.11-12.5 Analyze how an author's choices concerning how to structure specific parts of a text (e.g., the choice of where to begin or end a story, the choice to provide a comedic or tragic resolution) contribute to its overall structure and meaning as well as its aesthetic impact.
	W.11-12.3 Write narratives to develop real or imagined experiences or events using effective technique, well-chosen details, and well-structured event sequences.
	W.11-12.5 Develop and strengthen writing as needed by planning, revising, editing, rewriting, or trying a new approach, focusing on addressing what is most significant for a specific purpose and audience. (Editing for conventions should demonstrate command of Language standards 1–3 up to and including grades 11–12 here.).
	W.11-12.10 Write routinely over extended time frames (time for research, reflection, and revision) and shorter time frames (a single sitting or a day or two) for a range of tasks, purposes, and audiences.
	L.11-12.5 Demonstrate understanding of figurative language, word relationships, and nuances in word meanings.